The Guide to
National Parks
of the Southwest

ROSE HOUK

WESTERN NATIONAL PARKS ASSOCIATION
TUCSON, ARIZONA

The Guide to National Parks of the Southwest

UTAH
COLORADO
ARIZONA
NEW MEXICO
TEXAS

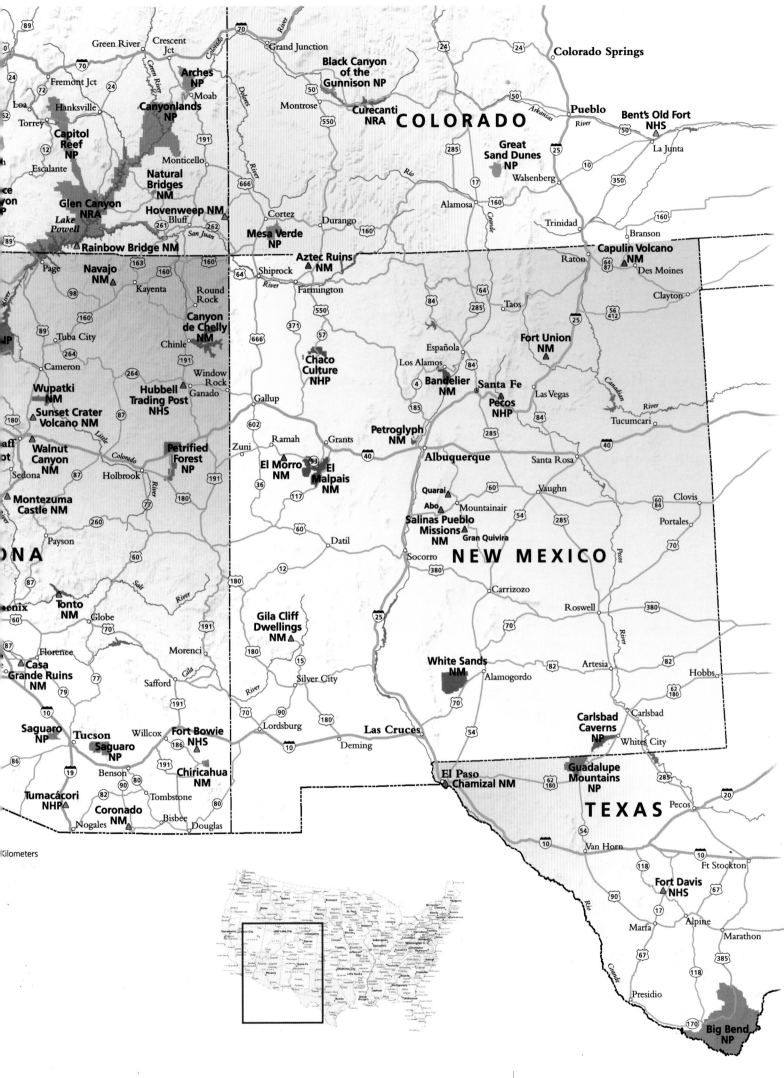

Introduction

Wallace Stegner, the dean of western writers, called the national parks "the best idea we ever had." And in the southwestern United States, with its astounding collection of national parks and monuments, that idea achieves finest expression. This guide covers fifty-two of those sites, each one different from the other, each with a unique geologic, biologic, historic, or archeologic story to tell. Some of them have attained international significance for the values they protect.

There are caves, canyons, rivers, deserts, mountains, frontier forts, Spanish churches, cliff dwellings, and million-acre wildernesses, all places of mystery and magic where the power of natural forces and human history can be directly witnessed and experienced. The parks and monuments of the Southwest offer visitors nearly endless opportunities to camp, hike, boat, bicycle, picnic, sightsee; chances to explore, learn, participate, and contemplate.

The Southwest's treasures were recognized early on. Casa Grande Ruins National Monument in central Arizona was the nation's first archeological preserve, established in 1892. Then, in 1906 President Theodore Roosevelt signed the Antiquities Act, which gave the president the authority to create national monuments that held "objects of historic or scientific interest." Though it would be another ten years before the National Park Service was created, Roosevelt moved quickly in the next two years and used the act to designate several monuments in the Southwest—Montezuma Castle, Chaco Canyon, Natural Bridges, Navajo, Tonto, Petrified Forest, Gila Cliff Dwellings, and Grand Canyon. Some have since become national parks. All are included here, as well as other national parks and monuments in a geographic area that stretches from west Texas, through New Mexico and Arizona, and into southern Utah and Colorado.

Through text and photographs, this guide describes each park and monument and gives practical information to help plan a visit. Once at a park, the visitor centers, museums, or contact stations always make a good first stop. Exhibits, audio-visual programs, and park rangers there provide valuable education and information. Many parks also offer living history demonstrations, nature walks, and evening programs to enhance a trip.

The information in the guide was current at the time of publication, but hours, facilities, and services can change. Visitors are advised to check individual parks on the National Park Service website at www.nps.gov. Each park's website also includes detailed information about weather. In general, the Southwest is a dry place. Humidity is low, sunlight is intense, and water sources are scarce. Summers in the desert parks are hot— daytime temperatures often exceeding 100 degrees Fahrenheit; winters are their prime seasons. Parks farther north, or at higher elevations, are more popular in summer. Some parks have such a great range of elevation within their boundaries that it's possible to find better weather just by changing altitude. Spring and fall are often windy and subject to sudden, unpredictable changes in weather.

Most parks charge an entrance fee, and many also have user fees. A National Park Passport, Golden Age Passport, or Golden Access Passport are good bargains. The parks belong to all of us and they are irreplaceable.

In the 76,000 acres of Arches National Park, some 2,000 natural arches have been catalogued, one of the greatest concentrations of these structures anywhere on earth.

Arches
NATIONAL PARK

ARCHES NATIONAL PARK
VISITOR INFORMATION

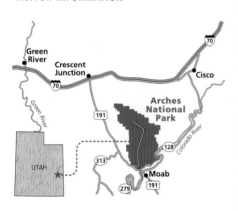

‹ OPEN › Year-round

‹ VISITOR CENTER › Open 8 a.m.–4:30 p.m., with extended hours spring through fall, closed December 25. Exhibits, orientation program, booksales

‹ ENTRANCE FEE › Yes

‹ CAMPING › Devils Garden Campground open all year, first-come, first-serve, additional sites on adjoining Bureau of Land Management lands

‹ SERVICES I FACILITIES › Picnic areas, restrooms, drinking water; no lodging, food, or gasoline in park

‹ NEARBY ACCOMMODATIONS I SERVICES › Moab, Utah

‹ INFORMATION › Superintendent, Arches National Park, P.O. Box 907, Moab, UT 84532; phone: 435-719-2299; website: www.nps.gov/arch

Swirled slickrock, slabbed fins, ponded potholes, pointed pinnacles, and finally, the pièce de résistance, curvaceous arches. In the 76,000 acres of Arches National Park, some 2,000 natural arches have been catalogued, one of the greatest concentrations of these structures anywhere on earth. They come in all shapes and sizes, from small whimsical openings just being born to the mature likes of Landscape Arch, whose elegant 306-foot span ranks it as one of the longest arches in the world. There's Delicate Arch, the icon of the park, that so perfectly frames the snow-capped La Sal Mountains you're hard pressed to accept it as a mere accident of nature.

Why so many arches here in this corner of southeast Utah? The answer rests in sandstone sitting on a bed of salt. The salt was deposited in an ocean about 300 million years ago and was then covered with more layers of sediment that were cemented into rock up to a thousand feet thick. The pressure exerted by this weight caused the salt to flow like warm taffy, doming up in places and collapsing in others. The younger upper layers were peeled away down to the Entrada Sandstone, the rock in which nearly all the arches have formed. Faulting aided the formation of cracks and joints in the Entrada, providing entryways for water.

Repeated freezing and thawing of water pried apart the sandstone into parallel fins, beautifully featured in the park's Fiery Furnace area. The fins were like stone tablets, waiting for water and wind to write on them. Flakes and chunks of rock sloughed away in weak spots, and with the help of gravity the openings grew into arches. Usually slow and patient, the process can at times be

impetuous and catastrophic. In 1940, Skyline Arch doubled in size with one rockfall. In September 1991 Landscape Arch enlarged with great fanfare when a 70-foot-long slab—some 180 tons of rock—shattered to the ground before the eyes of stunned hikers.

The arches and other geologic curiosities stand amid a high desert, ranging from 4,000 to 5,600 feet in elevation. Shrubby gray blackbrush and golden grama grasses dot the sandy terrain, along with fragrant Utah juniper and piñon pine. Cottonwood, single-leaf ash, and non-native tamarisk edge Courthouse and Salt washes.

Nearly everywhere, the ground is covered with an unassuming-looking, but highly valuable, plant community. Nearly invisible in its early stages, this substance called cryptobiotic crust matures into a dark-colored, hummocky material. Though it appears dead, the crust is a living concoction of cyanobacteria (blue-green algae) and lichen, mosses, fungi, and bacteria. The cyanobacteria weaves a web of filamentous fibers that bind the soil, help fix nitrogen, store water, and add organic material to the soil. "Cryptos," for short, is vital stuff in this

desert. It holds the soil in place and provides a seedbed from which other plants arise. Scars from boot prints or tire tracks can take decades, possibly centuries, to heal, which is why park visitors are implored not to "bust the crust."

Wildlife seem elusive in the park, but tallies tell otherwise—53 species of mammals, including mule deer; kit fox; coyote; jackrabbits; rodents; and desert bighorn sheep, exciting animals now seen since their successful reintroduction into the canyon country. More than 185 bird species have been observed in Arches, with pinyon jays, ravens, turkey vultures, juncos, hawks, and sparrows among the more common ones. Twenty-one reptile species, six different amphibians, and an untold number of insects are also counted in the inventory.

Few people have lingered here. Ten thousand years ago, hunters stopped along Courthouse Wash long enough to chip stone points from hard chalcedony. Ancestral Puebloans and their Utah contemporaries, the Fremont, left behind clay pottery, stone tools, and chipped petroglyphs of gamboling bighorn sheep. But these people departed 700 years ago. Ute and Paiute arrived,

and when Spanish priests Domínguez and Escalante came through in 1776 they were still in the area. About the only full-time Anglo settler was one John Wesley Wolfe, whose 1890s log cabin still stands along the trail to Delicate Arch. A Moab doctor, a newspaper editor, and a prospector who were especially fond of the place finally convinced President Herbert Hoover to declare Arches National Monument in 1929. After further expansions, Arches became a national park in 1971.

Opposite Above: Skyline Arch
Opposite Below: Delicate Arch, one of 2,000 natural arches preserved
Below: Courthouse Wash often floods after rainfall.

To modern–day Puebloans, Aztec was a home of their ancestors known as the "Place by Flowing Waters."

Aztec Ruins
NATIONAL MONUMENT

AZTEC RUINS NATIONAL MONUMENT
VISITOR INFORMATION

❮ **OPEN** ❯ Year-round except Thanksgiving, Christmas, and New Year's days

❮ **VISITOR CENTER** ❯ Open 8 a.m.–6 p.m. Memorial Day through Labor Day; 8 a.m.– 5 p.m. rest of year. Exhibits, books, movie

❮ **ENTRANCE FEE** ❯ Yes

❮ **CAMPING** ❯ No

❮ **SERVICES | FACILITIES** ❯ Restrooms, water, picnic area

❮ **NEARBY ACCOMMODATIONS | SERVICES** ❯ Food, gasoline, lodging in Aztec and Farmington, New Mexico. Camping at Navajo Lake State Park, Angel Peak Recreation Area, and commercial campgrounds

❮ **INFORMATION** ❯ Superintendent, Aztec Ruins National Monument, 84 County Road 2900, Aztec, NM 87410; phone: 505-334-6174, TDD dial ext. 30; website: www.nps.gov/azru

Although Aztec Indians never lived here, Aztec Ruins National Monument in northern New Mexico shows an outstanding example of the ancestral Puebloans who did live in the area. They knew a good thing when they saw it, gravitating to the Animas River, a perennial water source.

The residents did take advantage of the river to water their crops, but Aztec was much more than a humble farming community. By all accounts, it was a deliberately planned complex of public structures and a variety of other intriguing buildings and features. Among them are three "great houses," at least a half dozen large ceremonial structures called great kivas, many smaller kivas, and some thirty small pueblos. Also present are three "tri-wall" structures—aboveground kivas encircled by three concentric walls. The land was modified with berms, earthen pedestals beneath structures, and linear swales marking numerous roads in the area.

The fullest revelation of Aztec's story began in 1916 when the American Museum of Natural History hired a young local man named Earl Morris to head excavations. By then the site was surrounded by alfalfa fields, and livestock and picnickers visited the rubble-filled rooms.

In the West Ruin, Morris and his crew cleared away tons of shrubs and debris and dug, sifted, and repaired the site. The West Ruin—a three-story building of nearly 400 rooms—showed a relationship to Chaco Canyon fifty miles south, which flourished in the A.D. 1000s. The architecture was very similar to the massive, finely crafted sandstone slab veneer-and-core style used at Chaco. The West Ruin's formal layout indicated careful planning. Dates on tree rings from wood beams suggest two major periods of harvesting and stockpiling timbers beginning in 1109, each followed by intense construction episodes that concluded about 1130. Construction on a second great house—now called the East Ruin—occurred at the same time, but took almost 150 years to complete.

During Morris's seven field seasons, thousands of artifacts were recovered: mounds of pottery, bushels of corn, stacks of raw goods such as cottonwood slabs and clay, bone and stone tools, woven sandals, cotton cloth, cradleboards, and fine rings, bracelets, pendants, and bead jewelry made from exotic shell and turquoise.

Recent interpretations suggest one continuous, persistent occupation at Aztec over nearly two centuries. Although drought conditions slowed construction at the East Ruin for a time, building resumed when conditions improved. Adhering to a grand blueprint, the complex was completed during the late 1200s. Changes during the later Mesa Verde period may have evolved in place or been transmitted as ideas, rather than a change in the people who lived there.

Aztec became a national monument in 1923, with Morris as custodian.

In 1934 Morris began to reconstruct the Great Kiva in the plaza of the West Ruin. This round, semisubterranean chamber is immense— nearly fifty feet in diameter. Morris called the kiva an "intricate sanctuary," a central gathering place where people met for elaborate religious ceremonies, social events, or public business.

To modern-day Puebloans, Aztec was a home of their ancestors known as the "Place by Flowing Waters." It is a special place, writes Greg Cajete, a member of the Santa Clara Pueblo, because it shows the ingenious way the ancestral Puebloans lived in this environment and because it "exemplifies the spirit of place and community which Pueblo people have always treasured."

Above: Earl Morris reconstructed the Great Kiva in 1934.

It was the steady supply of flowing water that likely brought people to this place. Water's importance is expressed in a zigzag pictograph painted in black on a rock wall.

techniques in response to the vagaries of the semi-arid climate, where average yearly moisture is only about fifteen inches. They had a good understanding of the growing season here at 6,000 feet and knew which seeds to save for next year's crop. They dug irrigation canals and planted gridded gardens. They also had a long history of ceremony to assure fertility and abundance.

In their fields, the Puebloans grew the traditional southwestern crops of corn, beans, and squash. They also enjoyed the lush wild resources along Frijoles Creek and took advantage of game animals and wood up on the plateau. They made clay pottery, especially a later, beautiful glazeware. To get those things they could not grow or make themselves, they traded with others. The nearby Jemez Mountains contained a source of obsidian, a valuable glassy-black volcanic rock that was swapped for items such as macaws from the south.

After four centuries of successful habitation, though, the ancestral Puebloans left the area. By the late 1500s, when the Spaniards settled in New Mexico, they had vacated the Frijoles watershed and Pajarito Plateau. With resources exhausted, the Native people likely moved to villages along the

Below: Cavate dwellings
Bottom: The kiva in Ceremonial Cave

Bandelier
NATIONAL MONUMENT

Frijoles Creek slices a deep canyon through the Pajarito Plateau before it joins the Rio Grande in northern New Mexico. Though the plateau's volcanic tuff was too soft for building stone, early Pueblo people found the natural cavities eroded in the porous rock walls nicely suited for shelter. They successfully enlarged these Swiss-cheese-like openings by hand, laying up masonry walls and using the alcoves themselves as the back walls of the dwellings.

The ancestral Puebloans moved south from the Four Corners region and occupied what is now known as Bandelier National Monument from A.D. 1150 to the 1500s. They enjoyed a classic period here during the 1400s, when population peaked. During these centuries, they built Tyuonyi Pueblo at the bottom of Frijoles Canyon, as well as Long House and other cavate dwellings and talus villages at the base of the cliffs. Tsankawi and four other large villages on the northern part of the plateau also date to this period. While many people were coming together in larger villages, other families continued to live in smaller homesteads among the pines and junipers. With nearly three-fourths of Bandelier's 33,000 acres surveyed, thousands of archeological sites have been recorded.

It was the steady supply of flowing water that likely brought people to this place. Water's importance is expressed in a zigzag pictograph painted in black on a rock wall. It likely depicts a feathered serpent, a being traditionally associated with water in the Pueblo world.

By the time the ancestral Puebloans migrated into this part of the world, they already were accomplished farmers. They employed a host of

Rio Grande. Today's residents of Cochiti and San Ildefonso pueblos consider themselves descendants of Bandelier's early dwellers.

The region's archeological wealth began to come to the public's attention in the late nineteenth century. Anthropologist Adolph Bandelier arrived in the fall of 1880, with Cochiti guide Juan Jose Montoya. Deeply impressed, Bandelier wrote scientific reports of his finds and penned a novel entitled *The Delight Makers* about the ancient people. When the national monument was created in 1916, it was named for him.

In the early 1900s, archeologist Edgar Lee Hewett spent several field seasons at Bandelier. He and his coworkers excavated Tyuonyi, uncovering nearly 400 rooms built in an oval shape around a central plaza. This excavated site is what visitors first see on the Main Loop Trail. Hewett also studied the so-called "talus villages," the small masonry pueblos on the slope above Tyuonyi. Bandelier's cultural treasures moved Hewett to write: "History is stored away in the archives of Mother Earth… written unconsciously in things fashioned for use and in things that ministered only to the satisfaction of the spirit…"

BANDELIER NATIONAL MONUMENT
VISITOR INFORMATION

《 OPEN 》 Year-round except Christmas and New Year's days

《 VISITOR CENTER 》 8 a.m.–6 p.m. summer, 8 a.m.–4:30 p.m. winter, 9 a.m.–5:30 p.m. spring and fall; exhibits, slide program, book-sales; Frijoles Canyon and Tsankawi open dawn to dusk

《 ENTRANCE FEE 》 Yes

《 CAMPING 》 Juniper Campground near park entrance open year-round weather permitting, tents and RVs (no hookups), first-come, first-serve; Ponderosa Group Campground by reservation; back-country camping with permit

《 SERVICES | FACILITIES 》 Restrooms, water, picnic area, snack bar, and gift shop

《 NEARBY ACCOMMODATIONS | SERVICES 》 Food and gasoline in Los Alamos and White Rock, New Mexico

《 INFORMATION 》 Superintendent, Bandelier National Monument, 15 Entrance Rd., Los Alamos, NM 87544; phone: 505-672-3861; website: www.nps.gov/band

Above: Paths worn into the volcanic tuff of Frijoles Canyon
Right: Upper Falls, Frijoles Creek

It was the only place between Independence, Missouri, and Santa Fe where travelers could rest and resupply.

Bent's Old Fort
NATIONAL HISTORIC SITE

BENT'S OLD FORT NATIONAL HISTORIC SITE
VISITOR INFORMATION

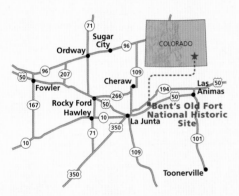

《 OPEN 》 Year-round, except Thanksgiving, Christmas, and New Year's days

《 HOURS 》 Fort open 8:00 a.m.–5:30 p.m. June through August; 9:00 a.m.–4:00 p.m. September through May. Guided tours in summer four times a day, two times a day in winter; self-guided tours also available; living history demonstrations; orientation film

《 ENTRANCE FEE 》 Yes, includes guided tours

《 CAMPING 》 No; nearest at John Martin Reservoir

《 SERVICES | FACILITIES 》 Restrooms, water, picnic area, bookstore and traderoom

《 NEARBY ACCOMMODATIONS | SERVICES 》 La Junta and Las Animas, Colorado

《 INFORMATION 》 Superintendent, Bent's Old Fort National Historic Site, 35110 Highway 194 East, La Junta, CO 81050; phone: 719-383-5010; website: www.nps.gov/beol

Though only a building of mud and straw, Bent's Fort must have looked like a castle to trail-weary travelers on the Great Plains. The large tan edifice, the largest structure of its kind between Missouri and New Mexico, became a center of commerce and community in the 1830s and 1840s.

Two brothers from St. Louis, Charles and William Bent, determined that money could be made trading goods from the East for beaver and buffalo pelts from the West. With Ceran St. Vrain, the Bent brothers formed Bent, St. Vrain and Company. The merchants heeded the advice of a Cheyenne leader, who suggested they locate a trading post on the Arkansas River in what is now eastern Colorado. In 1833, they began construction of their "mud castle" on the north side of the river, on a bench that afforded a wide view up and down the cottonwood-lined stream that then marked the boundary between the United States and Mexico.

The building was roughly rectangular, 137 feet by 178 feet, with adobe walls three to four feet thick. The heavy entry gate faced north. Two round towers rose at the northeast and southwest corners. All the rooms faced inward on a big central plaza, where a fur press occupied the center and flamboyant peacocks roamed at will. A kitchen, dining room, council room, and warerooms were on the ground level. On the second story were living quarters, along with an ornate billiard room well stocked with fine French wines. Muslin curtains provided thin privacy between rooms, and the exterior wood doors were weatherstripped with buffalo fur. The blacksmith and carpenter shops were always busy, and corrals at the rear of the building enclosed Spanish Barb horses, tough oxen, and Dominique chickens.

"Bent's Big Lodge," as it was sometimes known, was well situated along the mountain route of the Santa Fe Trail. From St. Louis came wagonloads of calico, canned coffees and teas, tinware, and tobacco. Trappers and mountain men brought in beaver skins. As the beaver were trapped out, Cheyenne and other Plains Indians substituted buffalo hides, which became the main item of exchange at the fort.

In late autumn and into winter, Bent's Fort hummed with activity. After the trader engaged in elaborate ritual with the Cheyenne, Arapaho, and others for the hides, appropriate payment was made in coveted imports.

Although foremost a trade center, it was the only place between Independence, Missouri, and Santa Fe where travelers could rest and resupply. Forty to sixty people were employed at the fort, and a parade of visitors passed through.

By 1846, the days of Bent's Fort were numbered. Charles Bent, then governor of New Mexico Territory, was killed in an uprising in Taos. In 1849, after only sixteen years of operation, the fort was abandoned, burned, and left to ruin.

Today, visitors see a full-scale reconstruction completed in 1976 by the National Park Service.

Above: The plaza at Bent's Old Fort

Big Bend is far from almost anywhere. That remoteness and isolation have, in many ways, served as its salvation.

Big Bend
NATIONAL PARK

Black bears and lizards. Cactus and oaks. Warblers and hawks. Bone-dry washes and flood-warning signs. Everything about Big Bend National Park speaks of extremes. In this 1,100-square-mile park, startling contrasts abound.

Named for its location, Big Bend sits in the crooked elbow of the Rio Grande as it demarcates the international border between west Texas and Mexico. Along this 118-mile stretch, the river has incised a trio of deep, gorgeous canyons—Santa Elena, Mariscal, and Boquillas.

Nearly all the park is desert, yet overall the color of the land is surprisingly green, even in the driest times. Rising out of the lowlands are wild, tortured hills and mountains, the most impressive of which are the Chisos Mountains in the core of the park. Sheer cliffs, flat-topped mesas, and scrawling arroyos add to the scenery. Elevation extends from 1,800 feet at the river to more than 7,800 feet on Emory Peak, the park's highest point. Big Bend is far from almost anywhere. That remoteness and isolation have, in many ways, served as its salvation.

Nearly endless exploration is possible on trails and backroads and along the river. One of the park's big attractions is bird life—nearly 450 species have been observed. Turkey vultures rise on thermals and circle over the broad desert valleys, joined by the occasional zone-tailed hawk or golden eagle. Cactus wrens chatter in the prickly pear and cholla, while acorn woodpeckers industriously stash acorns in holes in tree trunks. Many of the birds are migrants passing through in spring and fall, following the corridor of the Rio Grande. Down at Rio Grande Village in late April and early May,

the green cottonwoods are alive with flashes of red: vermilion flycatchers, tanagers, finches, cardinals. Warblers add dashes of yellow, painted buntings splashes of blue. Throughout the park, birders peer through binoculars and spotting scopes, awaiting a glimpse of the really rare ones, like the coveted Colima warbler or Lucifer hummingbird. Many of these avian migrants come from Mexico and Central America, some from as far away as South America. The Colima warbler and others summer in the higher elevations of Big Bend, breeding and bearing young, while others continue their epic movements farther north.

The plant roster of Big Bend, more than a thousand species, likewise offers some interesting members. The park protects the largest expanse of Chihuahuan Desert in the United States; its signature plant here is the stiff-leaved, needle-sharp lechuguilla. It often grows with a close lookalike, called *Hechtia,* or Texas false agave, that edges just across the border from Mexico. On the river floodplain and at springs, cottonwoods, willows, and cane luxuriate with the blessing of water. Resinous creosote bush, with tarbush, ceniza, and whitethorn acacia, account for thousands of acres of shrub desert. The sotol-grassland community covers another half of the park. Sotol's tall flowering stalks spear the blue sky, earning it the name desert candle. Grama and tobosa grasslands were once more extensive but suffered during heavy grazing in the nineteenth century. A little higher up find a tiny but no less significant woodland community of oak, piñon, juniper, Texas madrone, and in a few places bigtooth maples and Arizona cypress.

Good spring rains bring an explosion of wild-

flowers—bluebonnets line the roads, luscious creamy-white flowers hang on the Spanish dagger yuccas out on Dagger Flats, and jewel-like blossoms adorn hedgehog and prickly pear cactus. Big Bend is especially rich in members of the cactus family, with more than sixty different kinds known in the park. Prolific late summer rains usher in a colorful repeat bloom: mountain sage and scarlet bouvardia in showy reds; gentians, rosemallows, and tansy asters adding purple, pink, and yellow.

Relics and crossovers tell intriguing ecological stories in Big Bend. Spotted chirping frogs, quaking aspen, Douglas fir, and the little Carmen white-tailed deer are relics from a time, 8,000 years ago and more, when the climate was much cooler; they have found refuge in the higher Chisos Mountains. The same is true for black bears, which are native to Big Bend and were common in the early 1900s. The present population of about a dozen bears has been traced to one or two females that crossed the Rio Grande from Mexico and wandered into the park in the 1980s. These "Tex-Mex" bears, as they're fondly called, cross back and forth on the border as conditions warrant. The bears' reappearance contributes an exciting element to Big Bend's ecosystem, but all visitors must constantly be vigilant, stashing food, drinks, cooking utensils, even toiletries in car trunks or in the bearproof storage lockers in the campgrounds.

Big Bend has seen radically different environments through time. The oldest rocks now exposed in the park are about 300 million years old. Seas covered this part of Texas for a couple hundred million years, leaving behind sediments that were cemented into sandstones and limestones. As the oceans receded, swamps and riverbeds became home to dinosaurs like the plant-eating *Alamosaurus,* whose huge vertebrae have been unearthed in the park. About 70 million years ago, as the land began rising, the skies were home to the amazing *Quetzalcoatlus,* a pterosaur with a thirty-five-foot wingspan. Things were quiet for a bit, then a series of violent volcanic eruptions

Above Left: The Río Grande
Above: The Chisos Mountains
Right: Cactus wren
Far Right: Claret cup hedgehog cactus

began to rock the region about 50 million years ago, spewing ash and lava across the land, making the Chisos Mountains and many other topographic features look freshly fired. With cooler times during the Ice Age, animals such as the hippolike *Coryphodon,* turtles, crocodiles, garfish, and four-toed horses inhabited Big Bend.

Human beings didn't come onto the scene until about 10,000 years ago, leaving behind only a few hunting tools. Spaniards arrived in the 1500s and called this the *despoblado,* or uninhabited land. It was a misnomer, though, for the Jumanos Indians were living here then. Spanish traders established the Camino Real from Mexico City, to Chihuahua, to El Paso, and all the way to Santa Fe. Apaches were an ever-present force, and conflicts arose. Finally, in 1791 a peace was declared and the Spaniards left Big Bend to the Apache and Comanche. The territory fell first to Mexico, and then to the United States in 1848. Government surveyors tried to mark the international border accurately but found navigation of the Rio Grande through Big Bend one of their biggest obstacles. Robert T. Hill, with the U.S. Geological Survey, finally completed the daunting task in 1899.

Ranchers entered in the late 1800s. They set up livestock operations down on the Rio Grande or at cottonwood-shaded springs like Dugout Wells. Overgrazing knocked back the grasslands for a time, but they now appear to be coming back in places. A Chihuahuan plant called can-dellila supported another industry in the early twentieth century. The plant was harvested, carried

to factories at Glenn Springs and elsewhere on the backs of burros, then the wax was extracted. Wax camps still operate on the Mexico side of the Rio Grande.

Remote and enticing, Big Bend is filled with endless human and natural history stories.

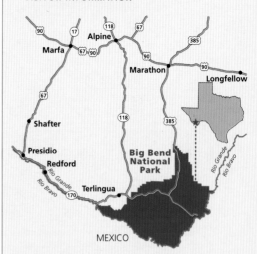

BIG BEND NATIONAL PARK
VISITOR INFORMATION

《 OPEN 》 Year-round, with limited hours Christmas Day

《 VISITOR CENTERS 》 Panther Junction 8 a.m.–6 p.m. all year; Chisos Basin 8 a.m.–4 p.m., shorter hours in winter; both have exhibits and book sales. Rio Grande Village 9 a.m.–4:30 p.m. November through April, closed in summer; exhibits and book sales.
Persimmon Gap open all year. Castolon Ranger Station open but not staffed full-time

《 ENTRANCE FEE 》 Yes

《 CAMPING 》 Rio Grande Village; Rio Grande Village RV Park (only campground with hookups); Chisos Basin (tents and smaller RVs); Cottonwood Campground near Castolon. All campgrounds first-come, first-serve. Also nearly 100 designated backcountry sites with primitive camping, require free permit from visitor centers

《 SERVICES | FACILITIES 》 Food and camping supplies at Chisos and Rio Grande Village; showers and laundry at Rio Grande Village store; gasoline at Panther Junction and Rio Grande Village; motel and restaurant at Chisos Mountains Lodge at the Basin

《 NEARBY ACCOMMODATIONS | SERVICES 》 Marathon, Alpine, Marfa, Study Butte, Terlingua, and Lajitas, Texas

《 INFORMATION 》 Superintendent, P.O. Box 129, Big Bend National Park, TX 79834; phone: 432-477-2251; website: www.nps.gov/bibe

Below: Strawberry cactus blooms in the foothills of the Chisos Mountains
Below Right: The post office in the Hot Springs Historic District

Colorado is graced by Black Canyon, one of the deepest, steepest canyons on the continent. At Warner Point on the South Rim, the chasm is 2,772 feet deep.

Black Canyon
OF THE GUNNISON NATIONAL PARK

That first view of the deep, dark gorge of Black Canyon of the Gunnison will steal a person's breath away. At the very bottom flows a tiny ribbon of clear, green water, the stream that carved this remarkable chasm.

The Gunnison River is the agent responsible for creating Black Canyon. And it took only about two million years to perform the task—a flash in the pan compared to the age of the rock through which the river cut. The craggy brown, gray, and black cliffs are nearly two billion years old. It's the basement of the earth, some of the oldest rock anywhere, transformed underground by extreme heat and pressure into metamorphic gneisses and schists hard as forged iron.

The formation of that ancient rock is the first chapter of Black Canyon's geologic story. Then, molten granite wedged into joints in the metamorphic rock. These pink and white streamers lend fascinating artistry to the slate-gray walls, showing to best effect on the 2,000-foot-high Painted Wall on the canyon's north side. Still, the schists and gneisses remained in the basement. Somehow that crystalline rock had to be exhumed and sliced through by the river.

About sixty million years ago, this core rock was warped up along with the entire Rocky Mountain region. Some thirty million years later, a period of riotous volcanic activity in the West Elk and San Juan mountains overlaid the block with basalt and ash. These volcanic caprocks controlled the course of the Gunnison. With renewed uplift that raised the schists to 8,000 feet above sea level, the now-entrenched river could only cut straight into the heart of the core. And so today western Colorado is graced by Black Canyon, one of the deepest, steepest canyons on the continent. At Warner Point on the South Rim, the chasm is 2,772 feet deep. And all of it has been exposed in a mere two million years.

The Gunnison could perform this mind-boggling feat because it once flowed with much greater volume. In springtimes the water crashed through Black Canyon sometimes at 12,000 cubic feet a second. Today, restrained by dams upstream in Curecanti National Recreation Area, the Gunnison's average flow has been reduced by two-thirds. Carried within that water was a prodigious load of sediment, the grinder that slowly chiseled away at the solid rock. That sediment also is being held behind the dams.

Black Canyon is so steep and deep partly because of the gradient of the Gunnison River. The river drops an average of forty-three feet a mile through Black Canyon, but in the park itself that descent increases precipitously, to ninety-five feet a mile. (In contrast, the average gradient of the Colorado River through Grand Canyon is eight feet a mile.) In a particular two-mile stretch, the Gunnison barrels down at 480 feet per mile. That kind of drop lends ferocious erosive power to the stream. In addition, the Gunnison has few regularly flowing tributaries coming in to widen the canyon.

The Ute, who called this part of Colorado home, apparently spent little time in the canyon; it presented too much of an obstacle to get through or across. Even the man for whom the river was named, Captain John Gunnison, struggled across the Lake Fork of the Gunnison, upstream of what is now the park in 1853. He probably never saw Black Canyon itself. Federal government surveyors with the Ferdinand Hayden party may have been among the first whites to view the gorge in 1873.

Above Right: The Gunnison River
Above Left: The Painted Wall marbled by granite

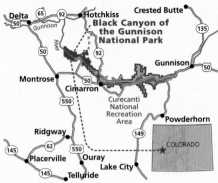

BLACK CANYON OF THE GUNNISON NATIONAL PARK
VISITOR INFORMATION

‹ OPEN › Year-round; South Rim Road open early April through mid-November, limited access in winter; North Rim open every day in summer, road and ranger station closed to vehicles in winter.

‹ VISITOR CENTER › Gunnison Point on South Rim open 8:30 a.m.–4 p.m. fall, winter, and spring, extended hours in summer. Closed Thanksgiving, Christmas, and New Year's days. Books, exhibits, audio-visual program

‹ ENTRANCE FEE › Yes

‹ CAMPING › South Rim Campground open year-round, North Rim campground open April to October; South Rim is much larger, with hookups at some sites

‹ SERVICES | FACILITIES › Restrooms and water

‹ NEARBY ACCOMMODATIONS | SERVICES › Food, gas, lodging and other services in towns of Montrose, Delta, Hotchkiss, and Paonia, Colorado

‹ INFORMATION › Superintendent, Black Canyon of the Gunnison National Park, 102 Elk Creek, Gunnison, CO 81230; phone: 970-641-2337; website: www.nps.gov/blca

But only in the winter of 1882-1883 do we have the first record of someone entering Black Canyon. They were surveyors for the Denver & Rio Grande Railroad, who labored for more than two months in the icy confines of the canyon to lay out a route for the tracks through this formidable terrain. The prohibitive cost led the company to take the railway up and out of the canyon.

A Montrose, Colorado, man, Will Torrence, was the first to attempt to navigate the Gunnison River through Black Canyon. In 1900, he and four other men set out in wooden boats to find a site for a tunnel to divert water from the river. The tortuous canyon forced them out. The next year engineer Abraham Lincoln Fellows hired Torrence, and the two returned with rubber mattresses and tried again. After nine long days Torrence and Fellows came to the end of their epic adventure. They had traveled thirty-three miles and lost fifteen pounds apiece. Despite the perils, the information they gathered launched the Gunnison Tunnel project, completed in 1909. The tunnel still carries water six miles to ranches and farms in the Uncompaghre Valley.

The muffled roar of white water on the Gunnison is audible from various places along the canyon rims. Marmots keep close watch from rimside boulders, and violet-green swallows and white-throated swifts blithely swoop out over the abyss. The forest on the rims consists mostly of piñon and juniper woodland, interspersed with groves of Gambel oak and serviceberry. Mule deer and elk browse shrubs, porcupines gnaw piñon bark, and the occasional black bear snuffles for acorns. Flickers and jays dart through the branches, and in summer saucer-sized flowers of arrowleaf balsamroot, pretty little bluebells, and bright paintbrush splash the ground.

A glance down the steep canyon slopes reveals tall evergreens and broadleaf trees. These are Douglas fir and aspen that take advantage of cooler, moister microclimates on the shadier walls. Down along the Gunnison yet another environment exists, a special world unto itself. Mountain willows, narrowleaf cottonwoods, and box elders shelter the immediate streamside, harboring warblers and

hummingbirds. Stoneflies hatch under rocks, trout rise up to snatch them, and ringtail cats come to the water for food. A person can spend hours watching the entertaining movements of the water ouzel, or American dipper, a bird that lives only where water flows fresh and sparkling.

A successful grassroots effort led to Black Canyon's designation as a national monument in 1933. In 1999 it became a national park of 30,380 acres, including fourteen of Black Canyon's total forty-eight miles.

Above: The Black Canyon contains some of the oldest rocks on earth.

Fairyland Point, Queen's Garden, Wall of Windows, Peek-a-boo Loop, Hat Shop, Silent City. The names alone suggest the Alice-in-Wonderland world that awaits in Bryce Canyon National Park. These monikers were stimulated by the weird and wonderful hoodoos, the proper geologic term for the fancifully eroded pillars of rock that decorate Bryce Canyon.

In truth, Bryce is not a canyon but an amphitheater carved into the east face of the Paunsaugunt Plateau in southern Utah. The bowl of the amphitheater is jammed with hoodoos in pastel pink, salmon, orange, white, and lavender. These statues of stone glow in the luminescent light of sunrise and sunset. And if you can lift your gaze from the spellbinding thousand-foot depths, the nearly infinite vistas into the distant rockbound wilderness of southeast Utah beg words of adequate description.

The Paunsaugunt Plateau is nearly the highest of a set of elevated tablelands called the High Plateaus of Utah. The plateaus occupy a geologic transition zone between the Colorado Plateau to the south and east and the Basin and Range to the west. Geologist Clarence Dutton, exploring these plateaus in the 1870s, called the Paunsaugunt escarpment the Pink Cliffs. Later, geologists determined that Bryce's origins were in a series of freshwater lakes and streams that collected sediments from higher ground some fifty to sixty million years ago. The limes, sands, and muds were cemented into inter-fingered layers of rock called the Claron Formation. The sediments were eventually compressed and lifted up with the rest of the Colorado Plateau, and later raised even further by faulting during the more recent formation of the Basin and Range.

> The bowl of the amphitheater is jammed with hoodoos in pastel pink, salmon, orange, white, and lavender.

Bryce Canyon
NATIONAL PARK

From Sunset Point, hoodoos sparkle in the winter sun.

Once all that colorful rock was exposed, nature set to work with a fine chisel. Water followed the paths of gullies, leaving protruding fins of rock. Cracks, or joints, in those fins provided weak spots where summer flash floods and ice could wedge them apart. Thus the fins were worn down to free-standing pinnacles and spires—colonnades, obelisks, columns, and buttresses in the words of Mr. Dutton.

The entrancing shapes of hoodoos arise from the fact that some rocks are hard, while others are soft. Hard rock erodes more slowly, soft rock more quickly. When these types are interlayered as they are at Bryce, we see forms like Thor's Hammer, with an indented middle and a more resistant cap.

Erosion is also gnawing back into the rim of Bryce. Streams on the east side of the Paunsaugunt gather into the Paria River, a tributary of the Colorado. The streams move headward, eroding the face of the amphitheater at a fast clip—one to four feet every hundred years. But not to worry. There's still time, a few million years at least, to enjoy the amazing hoodoo circus of Bryce Canyon.

The Scenic Drive features a number of viewpoints, rising ever higher until road's end at Yovimpa Point, just over 9,100 feet elevation. The short Bristlecone Loop Trail departs there, for a look at the venerable bristlecone pines that cling to the wind-ravaged rim. The park's oldest bristlecone—dated at 1,700 years—grows on the point. At these heights, with 200 inches of snow possible in winter, the bristlecones live among a boreal forest of blue spruce, white fir, and quaking aspen. At slightly lower elevations, Bryce's forests consist of tall, fragrant ponderosa pines with greenleaf manzanita at their feet. Lower still is found a woodland of piñon and juniper.

Utah prairie dogs, found only in south-central Utah, have been restored in the park. Uinta chipmunks beg for contraband crumbs. Clark's nutcrackers squawk in the treetops, as they glean seeds from cones. Blue grouse dine on the needles of spruce and fir. Rumpled porcupines gnaw bark off branches, and short-horned lizards sit stock still in perfect camouflage on the ground beneath.

Paiute names still exist in this land—Yovimpa, Panguitch, and Paunsaugunt, "place of the beavers." Paiute history says the hoodoos are the Legend People who Coyote turned to stone. The park, however, was named for Mormon settler Ebenezer Bryce. He and his wife Mary came here in 1874–1875 and built their home at the mouth of the canyon that now bears his name.

Bryce Canyon's scenic virtues became known to a wider world in the early 1900s. Forester J.W. Humphrey was a leading

BRYCE CANYON NATIONAL PARK
VISITOR INFORMATION

❰ OPEN ❱ Year-round; temporary road closures due to snow in winter

❰ VISITOR CENTER ❱ 8 a.m.–4:30 p.m., with extended hours in spring, summer, and fall. Closed Thanksgiving, Christmas, and New Year's days; exhibits, books, video

❰ ENTRANCE FEE ❱ Yes

❰ CAMPING ❱ North Campground open all year, tent and trailer sites (no hookups), reservations available in the summer, first-come, first-serve the rest of the year; Sunset Campground open May to October, tent and trailer sites, first-come, first-serve

❰ LODGING ❱ Bryce Canyon Lodge near rim, open April through October, contact Xanterra Parks and Resorts, 14001 E. Iliff Ave., Ste. 600, Aurora, CO 80014, phone 888-297-2757, www.xanterra.com. Dining room, gift shop, post office, horseback rides

❰ SERVICES | FACILITIES ❱ General store, showers, laundry near North Campground

❰ NEARBY ACCOMMODATIONS | SERVICES ❱ Ruby's Inn just outside park; full services also available in Panguitch and Tropic, Utah

❰ INFORMATION ❱ Superintendent, Bryce Canyon National Park, P.O. Box 640124, Bryce Canyon, UT 84764; phone: 435-834-5322; website: www.nps.gov/brca

promoter, along with Park Service director Horace Albright. By 1923, roads had been completed and travelers began to enter Bryce, Zion, and the other southeast Utah parklands. Bryce became a national monument in that year. The Utah Parks Company's rustic Bryce Canyon Lodge, designed by architect Gilbert Stanley Underwood of local stone and wood, was finished in 1925. Legislation to create Utah National Park passed in 1924, but a name change in 1928 created Bryce Canyon National Park.

Above: The Promontory from Rainbow Point

Above Right: Navajo Loop Trail

The Navajo call it *tseyi,* "place within the rocks." For them, nearly every rock in Canyon de Chelly possesses a name and holds significance: the place where they shot arrows into a crack in the rock, the rock where they played the hoop and pole game, the rock struck by lightning, the rock where the holy people sit.

Canyon de Chelly is not only the home of their holy ones, it is also home to the Diné, as the Navajo call themselves. They have lived amid the soaring sandstone walls for centuries, building their octagonal dwellings, called hogans, of logs and stone. They still grow corn, squash, and peaches in fields beside the streams, grandmothers in long tiered skirts walk up and down the trails, and the gentle ringing of sheep bells floats up to the rim overlooks.

> The Diné have lived amid the soaring sandstone walls for centuries, building their octagonal dwellings, called hogans, of logs and stone.

Canyon de Chelly
NATIONAL MONUMENT

As native Canyon de Chelly resident Wilson Hunter writes, "The opportunity to live and survive with the land is considered a gift from our holy people."

Canyon de Chelly and its major tributary, Canyon del Muerto, head to the east up in the forested Chuska Mountains and the Defiance Plateau of northeastern Arizona. Tsaile Creek flows down del Muerto, meeting the Rio de Chelly to form Chinle Wash. The canyon walls at Chinle are only about fifty feet high, but going upstream they rise ever higher to a sheer thousand feet.

It was the water in the washes, along with the farmable bottomlands, that drew the Navajo here. But others preceded them, perhaps by at least 1,500 years. There is evidence of inhabitants in the region as early as 200 B.C. They are known as Basketmakers for their fine woven basketry. They lived in pithouses, subterranean structures dug in the floors of the sweeping alcoves in the canyon walls. By about A.D. 500 their successors, the ancestral Puebloans, began to build multiroomed stone homes aboveground, but still beneath the overhangs of the rock shelters. The Puebloans left Canyon de Chelly by the 1300s but their descendants, the Hopi and people from the Jemez, New Mexico, area, lived or passed through for a brief time after that.

Above: Spider Rock
Left: White House, built by ancestral Puebloans more than a thousand years ago

CANYONLANDS NATIONAL PARK
VISITOR INFORMATION

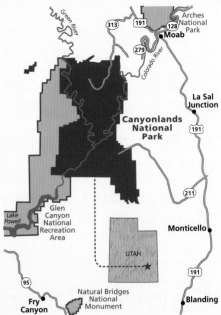

❰ OPEN ❱ Year-round

❰ VISITOR CENTERS ❱ Island in the Sky Visitor Center 8 a.m.–4:30 p.m. with extended hours during spring and fall, closed Christmas and New Year's days, open 8 a.m.–1 p.m. on Thanksgiving. Needles District Visitor Center, same hours and closures. Maze District (Hans Flat Ranger Station) same hours and closures, reachable on 46-mile dirt road. Exhibits, orientation programs, booksales

❰ ENTRANCE FEE ❱ Yes

❰ CAMPING ❱ Willow Flat Campground at Island in the Sky and Squaw Flat Campground in Needles, both open year-round, first-come, first-serve. Several designated camping areas on White Rim Road, permits required for all overnight trips, can be reserved in advance. Primitive backcountry camping throughout park, with permit.

❰ SERVICES | FACILITIES ❱ No food or lodging in park

❰ NEARBY ACCOMMODATIONS | SERVICES ❱ Moab, Monticello, and Green River, Utah

❰ INFORMATION ❱ Superintendent, Canyonlands National Park, 2282 S. West Resource Boulevard, Moab, UT 84532; phone: 435-719-2313; website: www.nps.gov/cany

world. Terra-cotta cliffs and soft brick-colored slopes stairstep down 1,500 feet to a white-edged platform that marks the final 1,000-foot drop into the river canyons themselves.

Entire oceans, rivers, and sandy deserts have come and gone, over the course of 300 million years or so, in what is now Canyonlands National Park. The oldest—the Paradox Formation—resulted from a shallow sea that repeatedly evaporated, leaving behind extensive saltbeds. Ensuing seas and rivers piled up thousands of feet of sands, silts, muds, and lime sediments. On top of these layers is the red-and-white banded Cedar Mesa Sandstone, into which the Needles have been carved, and above it the White Rim Sandstone, the distinctive, nearly unbroken light band that caps the edge of the inner canyons. Still younger rocks—Moenkopi, Chinle, Wingate, Kayenta, and Navajo Sandstone—form the stately buttes and mesas that flank side canyons and broad valleys throughout Canyonlands.

Around 15 million years ago, this great layer cake of rock was lifted up in concert with the entire Colorado Plateau. Then, running water performed magic in this dry land. The Green, the Colorado, and innumerable sidestreams, controlled by faults, folds, and joints, fashioned this geologic paradise called Canyonlands.

Even at the highest elevations of the park at Island in the Sky—around 5,000 to 6,000 feet—the land is lucky to receive 10 inches of moisture a year. Plants hold on for dear life—clumps of Indian ricegrass, tenacious sagebrush, gnarled junipers. And animals live where they can. Desert bighorn scramble over the rocky land with ease, mule deer graze in the spacious "parks," beetles embroider tracks on wet sand. Ever-present and ever-wily ravens and coyotes thrive under nearly any conditions. Snakes and lizards do well here too. Potholes dimple the slickrock, delicate environments for ephemeral creatures such as tadpole and fairy shrimp.

Humans adapted to the rigors of this land too. Horseshoe, or Barrier, Canyon, displays an astounding array of petroglyphs and pictographs thousands of years old. Roadside Ruin in the Needles is a granary where ancestral Puebloans stored their corn away from marauding rodents. Nearly every canyon within the Needles evidences the presence of these early people. Centuries later, cowboys like John "Sog" Shafer and Howard Lathrop ran cattle and sheep from the low country up onto Island in the Sky. The Ekkers wintered theirs in the Maze, while the Scorups and Somervilles headquartered at the Dugout Ranch in the Needles. In the 1950s, the Atomic Energy Commission improved the cattle tracks into something resembling roads so uranium miners could reach prospects and claims. Thus visitors today can drive the White Rim Road and the Shafer Trail, albeit holding their breath on some of the wildest curves.

Canyonlands has always been a tough land to get around in. Therein lies its beauty and interest, as a national park protecting some of the last best wilderness in the Lower 48.

Above Left: Mesa Arch, Island in the Sky District
Right Clockwise: The Colorado River runs through the park; evening primrose and coyote.

Capitol Reef has always been a far corner of the world.

Capitol Reef
NATIONAL PARK

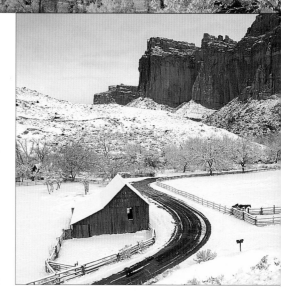

"It is the extreme of desolation, the blankest solitude, a superlative desert." So wrote geologist Clarence Dutton in the nineteenth century of the wild Waterpocket Fold country in southeast Utah. Dutton loved this place, as do most geologists, for here the bones of the earth are laid bare.

Capitol Reef National Park encompasses the Waterpocket Fold, a nearly hundred-mile-long swell of rock that winds sinuously from north to south. The "Fold," as it's known among locals, is a wrinkle in the otherwise flat-lying layers of the Colorado Plateau. It's like a big breaking wave, curling up on the east side then dropping steep and hard on the west face. It formed a barrier to travelers in the old days, who could get beyond it only by finding a through canyon—thus they called it a "reef." For the rounded domes of Navajo Sandstone that cap the Fold, the appellation "Capitol" was applied.

Capitol Reef is an open book of the Mesozoic era, the time of "middle life" that extended from 230 to 65 million years ago. Rivers, seas, and sands alternately left siltstones, mudstones, and sandstones. After those sediments were laid down, they were shoved up along what is likely an old, deeply buried fault. About 65 million years ago, the Laramide Orogeny began to put the big squeeze on this part of the world. This compression, which also raised the Rocky Mountains, pushed from both the east and the west, lifting the Waterpocket Fold nearly 7,000 feet. The Fold was raised again 20 to 17 million years ago, with renewed uplift of the entire Colorado Plateau. Erosion, mostly by water, stripped and molded the layers of rock and chewed into the heart of the Fold. Thus, this spec-

tacular Mesozoic section was revealed, rock in every shape, texture, and color—gray, buff, cream, mauve, and orange—soaring cliffs varnished with a coppery patina and clay slopes strewn with ripple-marked boulders.

In the more than 241,000 acres of Capitol Reef, people find canyons, gulches, arches, and dikes, secluded places where they can clamber over slickrock, elbow through tight spaces, and loll beside pockets of water in rock basins. That unfettered freedom to explore is the delightful essence of Capitol Reef.

The sighting of an animal, a wary coyote or a bat fluttering in the dusk, is an event. This is high desert, and animals are out mostly in early morning or evening. But they are here, coming to water to drink and exercising their freedom too. The park's wide elevation range—from more than 8,000 feet in the northwest corner down to around 4,000 at the southern end—and various soil types mean lots of habitats and lots of plant life: claretcup cactus, evening primrose, greenthread, globemallow, paintbrush, wire lettuce, box elder, buffaloberry, shadscale, rabbitbrush, piñon, juniper. Never lush, but all the same a fascinating botanical display of adaptability and endurance in the face of hot, dry summers and often bitter-cold winters.

Along with this scenic beauty, Capitol Reef also possesses a strong history of unique cultures who also adapted to the environment here. The Fremont River, the main watercourse that cuts from west to east through the Fold, lent its name to the Fremont Culture. Archeologist Noel Morss, working for the Peabody Museum, made finds here in 1928 and 1929 that indicated a culture

contemporaneous with, but distinct from, the Puebloans to the south and east. He observed rock-slab pithouses, plain gray pottery, exemplary rock art, clay figurines, and buckskin moccasins with the animals' dewclaws left on the soles, from which he defined the Fremont Culture. Archeologists have refined that definition through the years, but along the Fremont River in Capitol Reef visitors can still gaze upon fanciful petroglyphs pecked into the face of the Wingate Sandstone cliffs: birds, serpents, hunters, bighorn sheep leaping through the air, and bejeweled humanlike figures with elaborate headdresses.

The Fremont lived in the region from A.D. 700 until about 1300, and the reasons for their departure are not fully understood. Paiute and Ute hunters followed, and in the late 1870s and early 1880s a Euro-American group—members of the

CAPITOL REEF NATIONAL PARK
VISITOR INFORMATION

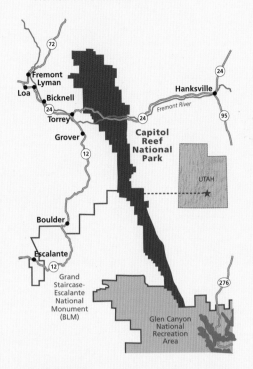

‹ OPEN › Year-round

‹ VISITOR CENTER › Open 8 a.m.–4:30 p.m. daily, extended hours in summer; closed some federal holidays. Exhibits, orientation program, bookstore

‹ ENTRANCE FEE › Yes

‹ HISTORIC DISTRICT › Fruita Schoolhouse, barns, orchards

‹ CAMPING › Fruita Campground, tents and RVs, first-come, first-serve. Primitive camping (no water) at Cathedral Valley and Cedar Mesa campgrounds. All three open year-round.

‹ SERVICES I FACILITIES › Water, restrooms, picnic areas; no lodging or other services in park

‹ NEARBY ACCOMMODATIONS I SERVICES › Full services in Torrey, Bicknell, and Hanksville, Utah

‹ INFORMATION › Superintendent, Capitol Reef National Park, HC 70 Box 15, Torrey, UT 84775; phone: 435-425-3791; website: www.nps.gov/care

Church of Jesus Christ of the Latter-day Saints—settled in.

As it was for the Fremont people, Utah was home for the Mormons. But the remote southeast quarter of the state was the last area they colonized. The Johnsons, Jorgensons, Behunins, Hanks, and Holts were among the stalwart pioneers who built homes and farms along the Fremont River. At most ten resourceful families formed the little burg of Junction, later renamed Fruita. Their barns, fields, orchards, and one-room school remain today in the park's historic district. And the fruit trees they planted—cherries, apricots, peaches, plums, and apples—still bear produce for the picking in summer and fall. Today the park's headquarters and main campground are located at Fruita too, where chukar and mule deer share the bucolic surroundings with campers.

Capitol Reef has always been a far corner of the world. The main thoroughfare along the Fremont River, Highway 24, wasn't paved until 1962. Up to that time, residents and travelers passed through the narrows of Capitol Gorge. Many felt compelled to leave evidence of their passage, carving their names on the cliff face. A short walk into the gorge leads to the Pioneer Register, where that history is recorded. After flash floods, men cleared away the mud and gravel to keep the route open. Others found they could expedite the Saints' colonization of southern Utah by ferrying them across the Colorado River. Halls Creek, which weaves along the east side of the Fold, was named for Charles Hall. From 1881 to 1884 he built and ran a ferry across what was then the Colorado River, now under the waters of Lake Powell.

Difficult though their journeys were, people have long looked at Capitol Reef as an Eden in the desert.

Opposite Above: In Fremont River Canyon cottonwoods frame the Castle.
Opposite Below: The Fruita historic district contains orchards, fields, and a one-room school.
Left: Peek-A-Boo Rock, Muley Twist Canyon

When it became a national monument, Capulin was characterized as "a striking example of recent extinct volcanoes . . . of great scientific and especially geologic interest."

Capulin Volcano
NATIONAL MONUMENT

Capulin Volcano saw a brief moment of glory about 60,000 years ago. The volcano itself is now extinct, but the elegant symmetrical cinder cone created by the eruption so inspired people that it became a small but significant national monument in 1916.

Rising some 1,300 feet above the wide, grass-filled plains of northeast New Mexico, Capulin is now preserved so that visitors can walk the crater rim and go down and peer into the vent whence the volcano was born.

The Capulin cinder cone built rapidly. Chunks of ash and cinders were hurled high into the air in a fantastic fireworks show. The cinders fell to the ground and accumulated until they reached their angle of repose, the point at which they stop sliding. Most cinder cones do not get any higher than Capulin. As the eruption was ending and much of the cone was built, hot lavas poured out of the base of the cone.

When it became a national monument, Capulin was characterized as "a striking example of recent extinct volcanoes . . . of great scientific and especially geologic interest." Indeed, the actual date of Capulin's eruption has been a matter of interest among geologists for quite some time. In the 1950s it was assigned an age of 10,000 years, a relative date based on a Capulin-emitted lava flow that was incorrectly correlated to the Folsom archeological site fifteen miles away. More recent, absolute dates obtained from chemical analyses indicate that Capulin's eruption was older—56,000 to 62,000 years. And because cinder cones form as one-time events, it's fairly certain that Capulin is now extinct.

The real drawing card at Capulin is the sensational scenery from the top of the crater, where four states can be seen. From the rim trail, you can gaze east to Sierra Grande floating out in the Plains ten miles distant, a shield volcano rising to 8,720 feet. You can also see Black Mesa in Oklahoma, the highest point in that state at 4,973 feet elevation. The Texas Panhandle is in sight, and out to the west more cones dot the landscape of New Mexico. On the farthest western horizon the glorious Sangre de Cristo Mountains, sometimes snow-capped, reach into Colorado.

The rim trail ascends to the highest point on the volcano—8,182 feet. Walkers, stopping to catch their breath, can appreciate the fact that southwest winds blew the cinders higher on the northeast side of the crater. Fragments of still-molten lava fell onto the rim and crater, fusing into what is called spatter. This coating has protected Capulin from eroding too quickly, as have shrubs and trees that have gained rootholds. The rusty boulders are splotched with chartreuse lichens, and skunkbush, Gambel oak, and chokecherry ("capulin" in Spanish) are bonsaied by the wind. Bluebirds, grosbeaks, and goldfinches flit through the trees, and in summer masses of ladybugs congregate on the plants. The short trail down into the 415-foot-deep crater puts you face to face with the volcano's rubble-filled vent.

CAPULIN VOLCANO NATIONAL MONUMENT
VISITOR INFORMATION

❰ OPEN ❱ Year-round except Thanksgiving, Christmas, and New Year's days

❰ VISITOR CENTER ❱ 7:30 a.m.–6:30 p.m. summer, 8 a.m.–4 p.m. in winter; park hours same as visitor center. Exhibits, video, books

❰ ENTRANCE FEE ❱ Yes

❰ CAMPING ❱ None on site; commercial RV park in town of Capulin with showers; Sugarite Canyon State Park near Raton, New Mexico, and Clayton Lake State Park outside Clayton, New Mexico

❰ SERVICES | FACILITIES ❱ Restrooms, water, picnic area

❰ NEARBY ACCOMMODATIONS | SERVICES ❱ Full services in Raton and Clayton, New Mexico

❰ INFORMATION ❱ Superintendent, Capulin Volcano National Monument, P.O. Box 40, Capulin, NM 88414; phone: 505-278-2201; website: nps.gov/cavo

Above: Capulin Volcano, part of the Raton-Clayton Volcanic field, which extends through northeastern New Mexico

Finally, after descending 750 feet into the earth, you emerge into the Big Room. This immense space, the largest natural limestone chamber in North America, forms the heart of Carlsbad Cavern.

A trip into Carlsbad Cavern leads into another world. If you go by way of the cave's natural entrance, you enter through a vaulted rock arch with cave swallows swooping and circling around you. The contrast is striking as you depart the bright desert glare and descend into the cool, dark cave.

As the steep trail switchbacks down, you look back up at the lens of daylight, dimming as you pass into the region known as the "twilight zone." The swallows are no longer your companions. Voices become whispers, and people pause and stare at the wonders. Only the added indirect lighting dispels the total darkness beyond the twilight zone.

The trail follows a large trunk passage called the Main Corridor. It leads past Devil's Spring, a mirror-clear reflective pool; Iceberg Rock, a 200,000-ton boulder that toppled from the cave ceiling; and the Boneyard, an uncompleted corner of the cavern. Finally, after descending 750 feet into the earth, you emerge into the Big Room. This immense space, the largest natural limestone chamber in North America, forms the heart of Carlsbad Cavern. Its cross-shaped layout covers about 9 acres, with a ceiling 255 feet high, dwarfing human scale. It contains a fantasyland of exquisite formations—delicate stalactites hanging down from the ceiling and stalagmites growing up from the floor. Other formations—pearls, popcorn, drapery, soda straws, lily pads, and gypsum flowers—adorn the cave, in colors of marble, alabaster, and brick.

After traversing the Main Corridor, some visitors may be eager to ride the elevator back up to terra familiar. But more awesome sights await in the Big Room, such as the spectacular Hall of the Giants, the black depths of the Bottomless Pit, the stalwart Rock of Ages, and the lovely Painted Grotto.

At the end of this three-mile, self-guided tour, you resurface into the "real world," forever

Carlsbad Caverns
NATIONAL PARK

Carlsbad Caverns, Papoose Room

wondering what else lies unseen beneath your feet. And it's only natural to begin to ask how this amazing underworld was created.

Limestone, water, microbes, and time are the key ingredients to making this cave. The building of the Capitan Reef was the first step. About 260 million years ago, the skeletons of sea creatures and precipitates from a shallow sea accumulated as a limestone "reef." Cracks and fissures developed in the rock, providing passageways that would eventually enlarge into caverns. As the ocean vanished and the reef stopped building, carbon-dioxide-rich rainfall formed a weak acid that entered and enlarged those fissures.

Next, that limestone reef had to be raised above sea level. This was accomplished through a major mountain-forming episode about 80 million years ago which lifted the Capitan Reef. Faulting and uplift, most recently during the Basin and Range upheaval 10 to 12 million years ago, resulted in the expression of a long, high mountain range—the Guadalupes—that stretches through west Texas into southeast New Mexico.

Still, researchers kept looking for something

else to explain how the Big Room got so big. They learned that single-celled microbes, called "extremeophiles," consumed carbon compounds in the oil reserves found in the Carlsbad region. In the process of "eating" oil, hydrogen sulfide was produced; this reacted with oxygen in the water table to yield sulfuric acid, much stronger than carbonic acid, strong enough to dissolve the vast amounts of limestone along fissures. As a by-product, it deposited the gypsum found in Carlsbad and other caves in the region. The sulfuric acid mixed inside the mountains, eating out ever larger, interconnecting spaces, forming Carlsbad Cavern about four to five million years ago.

An entire network of caves honeycombs the Guadalupes. Spelunkers and geologists are still finding new caves—the hundredth was just located within Carlsbad Caverns National Park, while another two hundred or so exist just outside the park boundaries.

After the big carving was done, most of the underground "acid bath" drained away. Then nature turned to the detail work, decorating the cave for a party. Water from rain and snow drained down,

dissolving limestone and then redepositing it in the caverns as calcite. This calcite is the primary material from which the speleothems—the cave formations—are made. The wettest time was about half a million years ago during the ice age, when drip-stones and flowstones were forming at a fast clip.

Today, because of the prevailing desert climate outside, Carlsbad is drying out. Still, the cave "breathes" with changes in atmospheric pressure. Temperature varies in places too, but the Big Room stays at a constant 56 degrees Fahrenheit. And life certainly dwells here. Bats, millipedes, mites, spiders, algae, fungi, cave crickets, and other animals and plants have adapted to this dark, cool world. A huge colony of Mexican free-tailed bats roosts in a section of the cavern in summer. Though varying from year to year, the population averages about half a million bats. Each evening at dusk they fly out by the thousands, heading for nearby water sources and feasting on insects.

People have known about the cave for at least 8,000 years, when American Indians lived in front of it. Euro-Americans also were aware of it. But it was bats that led the premier explorer to the cave.

Caver exploring Goat Cave

As the story goes, around 1898 a lanky cowboy named James White saw what looked like a curious plume of smoke spinning up from a hole in the ground. It wasn't smoke but the evening flight of masses of bats emerging from the cavern's natural entrance. White returned a few days later, fashioned a crude ladder, and dropped into the cave, using a homemade torch to light his way. Another local man, Abijah Long, was enticed by the amount of bat guano. He started mining it in 1903, with White as his foreman. The guano was lifted out by bucket and pulley and delivered by wagon to the railhead, bound for southern California as fertilizer for citrus trees.

The mining operation gave Jim White a perfect excuse to delve farther into the cave. Though he and Long soon split up (and both claimed credit as the "discoverer" of the cave), White was the one who introduced the wonders of the cavern to the public. He escorted photographer Ray V. Davis into the cavern, and in 1918 Davis took the first photographs of the Big Room. They appeared in the *New York Times* and fired people's interest in "the old bat cave." In 1923, geologist Willis T. Lee came with the support of the National Geographic Society. A year later, in October 1924, President Calvin Coolidge set aside Carlsbad Cave National Monument. Jim White was chief ranger briefly in the 1920s.

The Park Service installed trails, lights, and stairs, so visitors would no longer have to be hoisted up and down in guano buckets. Weddings and movies, the elevator and underground lunch room, all came to Carlsbad. It attained national park status in 1930 and later was expanded to encompass more than 46,000 acres. More than 35 million people have toured Carlsbad since 1923, and some hardier souls can still venture into the less developed rooms and other caves nearby.

And Jim White was right. Carlsbad Cavern is a sight everyone should see.

Above: Giant Dome, Hall of the Giants
Below: Bats fly at dusk

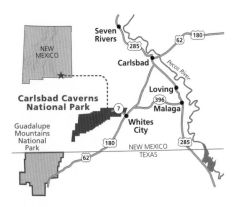

CARLSBAD CAVERNS NATIONAL PARK
VISITOR INFORMATION

❮ OPEN ❯ Year-round except Christmas Day

❮ VISITOR CENTERS ❯ Open 8 a.m.–5 p.m. Labor Day to Memorial Day; 8 a.m.–7 p.m. Memorial Day through Labor Day; exhibits, books, audio-visual program, ticket sales

❮ ENTRANCE FEE ❯ Yes, plus additional charges for interpretive cave tours and audio package

❮ CAVE TOURS ❯ Self-Guided—Big Room: 1 mile, easiest, elevator in and out, Kings Palace: 1 mile, moderate, elevator in and out

Natural Entrance: 1 mile one-way, most strenuous, steep paved trail descends 750 feet, elevator back out

Guided Off-Trail Routes—Special undeveloped cave tours with park guide:

Slaughter Cave: In summer, daily tours with park ranger, group size limited to 25; other off-trail tours include Lower Cave, Left Hand Tunnel, Hall of White Giant, and Spider Cave. Call visitor center or check website for more information.

For all tours wear non-skid, sturdy shoes and bring sweater or jacket. Constant temperature of 56 degrees in cave; baby strollers not allowed on cavern trails

Bat Flight Programs: At sunset each evening from mid-May through September, rangers conduct programs in the amphitheater at cavern entrance, as bats emerge for nighttime forays; very popular, arrive early for a seat

❮ CAMPING ❯ No developed campground in park. Backcountry camping possible with permit. Closest developed campgrounds in Guadalupe Mountains National Park, and towns of White's City and Carlsbad, New Mexico

❮ SERVICES I FACILITIES ❯ Restrooms, gift shop, restaurant, and kennel in visitor center; lunch counter and restrooms in cavern

❮ NEARBY ACCOMMODATIONS I SERVICES ❯ Gas, food, lodging in White's City and Carlsbad, New Mexico

❮ INFORMATION ❯ Superintendent, Carlsbad Caverns National Park, 3225 National Parks Highway, Carlsbad, NM 88220; phone: 505-785-2232. Cave Tour Reservations: 800-967-2283; website: www.nps.gov/cave

...the "great house" may have been used as an astronomical observatory, one of several ideas about the purpose of this enigmatic, imposing structure...

Casa Grande Ruins
NATIONAL MONUMENT

CASA GRANDE RUINS NATIONAL MONUMENT
VISITOR INFORMATION

《 OPEN 》 8 a.m.–5 p.m. daily except Christmas Day

《 VISITOR CENTER 》 8 a.m.–5 p.m.; closed Christmas; exhibits, books

《 ENTRANCE FEE 》 Yes

《 CAMPING 》 No

《 SERVICES I FACILITIES 》 Restrooms, drinking water, picnic area

《 NEARBY ACCOMMODATIONS I SERVICES 》 Coolidge and Florence, Arizona

《 INFORMATION 》 Superintendent, Casa Grande Ruins National Monument, 1100 Ruins Drive, Coolidge, AZ 85228; phone: 520-723-3172; website: www.nps.gov/cagr

At sunset, before the desert heat begins to ease, we can imagine this scene: The leader of the village retreats within the coolness of the Casa Grande. He watches patiently while the sinking sun just grazes a particular round opening in a high wall of the room.

Modern archeologists have observed such an alignment of the sun through a "window" in an upper room of the Casa Grande, marking the summer solstice. They have suggested that the "great house" may have been used as an astronomical observatory, one of several ideas about the purpose of this enigmatic, imposing structure that stands out in the desert of central Arizona. Others have seen the four-story building as a fort, a granary, or a silo. Whatever the truth, the Casa Grande's significance was recognized early on when it became the nation's first archeological preserve, in 1892.

While archeologists continue to add pieces to this puzzle, they have been able with more certainty to say who built the Casa Grande and when. The Hohokam, a major early culture of the desert Southwest, built the structure. Hohokam translates from the O'odham language as "those who have gone."

The Hohokam culture collapsed from the archeological record around A.D. 1450 after living successfully in this challenging environment since at least A.D. 300. They built brush-covered houses in pits, at first loosely arranged then placed in more organized villages around courtyards. They harvested the wild bounty of the Sonoran Desert— saguaro fruit, mesquite beans, mule deer, rabbits, turtles, and fish. Archeologists first defined the Hohokam as the "red-on-buff" culture, for their distinctive painted clay pottery. Through trade with neighbors to the south, they acquired more exotic items such as shell, macaw feathers, pyrite mirrors, and copper bells.

The most outstanding accomplishment of the Hohokam, however, was their mastery of the art of irrigation farming. They dug hundreds of miles of canals to divert water from two major rivers, the Salt and the Gila, and also constructed oval ballcourts and complex elevated platform mounds along the rivers—perhaps part of the administrative system that assured smooth working of their vast irrigation network.

The Classic Period of the Hohokam extended from A.D. 1100 to 1400. Toward the end of that period, in the 1300s, the Hohokam erected the Casa Grande. They added water to the local caliche soil to form a thick mud, kneaded the mud, then laid it up in courses without benefit of forms, eventually to nearly forty feet high. Three thousand tons of this mixture were used, which then dried to a rock-hard finish under the desert sun. More than six hundred wood beams, brought from mountains fifty miles away, were employed as roof supports. Yet after all that effort, the great house was used for only fifty to seventy-five years; it is one of only three similar buildings known in the area and is the only one still standing. Archeologists surmise that the end came, paradoxically, from prolonged drought followed by catastrophic floods in this dry land.

On a visit to Casa Grande you see not only the impressive great house itself, but also the melting mud walls of Compound A. These walls, which once stood nearly seven feet high, also once enclosed houses, work areas, courtyards, and storerooms. Near Compound A is an excavated ballcourt, where hundreds of people may have come together, perhaps after word went out that the setting sun was favorable for ceremonies to begin.

Above: The great house, protected by a roof built in 1932

Even in summer at these elevations the air carries a chill. But the rainbow-hued rocks and delightful meadows and forest invite leisurely exploration.

Cedar Breaks
NATIONAL MONUMENT

The season at Cedar Breaks is brief but glorious. This small national monument in southern Utah is open only in summer and early fall. In winter, deep snows cloak the 10,000-foot summits of the park.

Even in summer at these elevations the air carries a chill. But the rainbow-hued rocks and delightful meadows and forest invite leisurely exploration. The breathtaking "breaks," as they're called, are the precipitous, intricately carved slopes of a natural amphitheater three miles wide and 2,500 feet deep. The fins and spires and totems come in shades of white, russet, salmon, pink, and gray. Geologists know this as the Claron Formation, the same sedimentary rock of nearby Bryce Canyon

National Park, only here standing almost two thousand feet higher in elevation.

Because some sediments are softer and others are harder, weathering and erosion occur at different rates, creating the fantastic shapes of the spires. The palette of colors—changing subtly through the day and igniting at sunset—is due to varying amounts of minerals. Reds and oranges arise from iron content, limonite yields yellowish colors, and manganese oxides impart purples and blues.

The muds, silts, and limes of the Claron Formation were deposited in a freshwater lake some 50 to 60 million years ago, and millions of years later were raised along the faulted edge of

the soaring Markagunt Plateau. Cedar Breaks sits on the extreme western brink of the Markagunt, a Paiute word which means "highland of trees."

Those trees constitute the park's other great charm—an evergreen forest of Engelmann spruce and subalpine fir. Ancient, twisted bristlecone pines cling to windy ridgetops; one on Spectra Point is 1,600 years old. Meadows provide breaks in the wall of trees, brimming with alpine phlox, evening primrose, columbine, and lupine.

Steller's jays, Clark's nutcrackers, and ravens fly over those terraces. Fox, deer, marmots, mountain lion, and pikas inhabit this subalpine world. Some of these animals and plants were well known to the Southern Paiute, mainly desert folk who moved up to the high plateaus in summer. Later passersby, including Spanish friars and Anglo trappers, stayed mostly to the valleys where travel was easier. Pioneer settlers were hardy Mormons who applied the name Cedar Breaks to the juniper-dotted badlands. Notable among them was Charles Adams; his daughter ran a hotel at the north end of the park in the 1920s for tourists and townsfolk from Cedar City seeking refuge from the summer heat. Visitors arrived via the Union Pacific's spur rail line to Cedar City; the railroad's Utah Parks Company then drove people up to Cedar Breaks and on to the sister parks of Zion and Bryce Canyon. In 1933 Cedar Breaks attracted enough attention to become a national monument.

Above: Water, ice, and chemical and physical forces carved the rock formations.

In the arid open land of northwest New Mexico exists a fantastic collection of immense prehistoric buildings.

Chaco Culture
NATIONAL HISTORICAL PARK

For twenty miles along Chaco Wash in the San Juan Basin, nine "great houses," along with hundreds of other smaller sites, are protected within the bounds of Chaco Culture National Historical Park.

Lured by Chaco's reputation, visitors make the long drive over dirt roads to come and marvel at these structures—Pueblo Bonito, Chetro Ketl, Casa Rinconada, and others. Many people are struck too by a less easily defined quality—Chaco's evocative mystery. The exquisite sites inevitably inspire questions. What prompted the construction of these buildings? What was going on here in the ancestral Puebloan world a thousand years ago? After decades of research, archeologists have been able to answer some questions about Chaco, but they are still engaged in lively debate over others.

For sheer architectural achievement, the so-called great houses are unexcelled. The rock walls of some rise to five stories. Each building contains hundreds of rooms. The masonry is exacting and characteristic—a veneer of carefully worked, banded sandstones enclosing cores of rubble fill. A master design plan seems to have ruled their construction—foundations were stout enough to support the several additional stories, and overall the layouts assumed D- or L- shapes. Floor and ceiling beams were wood logs; an estimated 200,000 trees had to have been cut with stone axes and hauled in on people's backs from sixty miles away. Construction of the great houses began in the A.D. 860s and ended around 1130 to 1150.

With little evidence for living in many rooms of the great houses, archeologists label the structures as "public architecture." And though the resident population may have been relatively small,

archeologists have found an astonishing number of artifacts in some of the great houses. At Pueblo Alto on the mesa above Pueblo Bonito, a couple hundred thousand pieces of pottery, flaked stone, and food remains suggest lavish feasting or large religious or ceremonial gatherings. In addition to these intriguing finds, ceremonial spaces called kivas are plentiful at Chaco. Many are small, but a few are gargantuan. The great kivas at Chetro Ketl and Casa Rinconada are more than 60 feet in diameter and may have been the sites of region-wide ceremonies and events.

The climate and environment of Chaco and the San Juan Basin would have been challenging to farmers. The valley is at 6,200 feet elevation, and receives only about 9 inches of precipitation a year. Temperatures swing from sub-zero in winter to nearly 100 degrees Fahrenheit in summer. Yet there is plenty of evidence for cultivation. The floodplain was filled with fields and garden plots, watered by runoff channeled from the mesas and from irrigation canals. Whether the residents of Chaco grew enough to sustain themselves, or whether food had to be imported, remains a question.

Adding to Chaco's mystery is the system of roads that radiates in all directions. The roads are of varying widths and lengths—some are 30 feet wide and extend for more than 40 miles, take strikingly straight courses, and are bounded by earthen curbs and berms. A few have ramps and steps. Most roads lead to a number of sizable outlying villages that mimic Chaco architecture.

Chaco may have acted as the hub of a far-reaching trade network in the tenth and eleventh

Above Top: Pueblo Bonito contains more than six hundred rooms and thirty-three kivas.
Above: Effigy pottery, found at Pueblo Bonito

centuries. The "Chaco Phenomenon," as it's called, likely involved a complex social and political system based on importing and exporting valued goods, such as salt, copper bells, macaw feathers, pottery, and especially worked turquoise. The roads certainly provided a way for people and goods to come in and go out; they also may have controlled access and served as paths for ritual processions.

Culturally, Chaco achieved a zenith in the A.D. 1000s, with what must have been an enormous building boom in the canyon and far beyond. But by A.D. 1140 or so, construction of the great houses ceased. People still lived at Chaco for another hundred years or so, but on a much smaller scale.

After 300 years, why did the people give up the complex, centralized Chacoan system? The reasons are uncertain. Did the residents exhaust wood supplies and other resources? Was Chaco's role as a trade center superseded by other centers? Such questions remain part of the intriguing phenomenon known as Chaco.

Below: View of Fajada Butte from Chaco Canyon

CHACO CULTURE NATIONAL HISTORICAL PARK
VISITOR INFORMATION

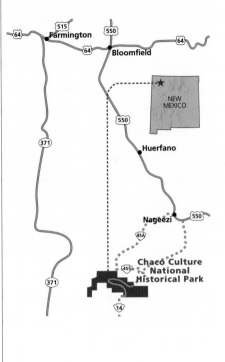

⟨ OPEN ⟩ Year-round; sites and trails open sunrise to sunset; all roads into park unpaved for good distances; recommended route in is Highway 550 near Nageezi, New Mexico; two other routes from south very rough and can be impassable in bad weather

⟨ VISITOR CENTER ⟩ Open 8 a.m.–5 p.m.; closed Thanksgiving, Christmas, and New Year's days; exhibits, films, astronomy observatory, booksales

⟨ ENTRANCE FEE ⟩ Yes

⟨ CAMPING ⟩ Gallo Campground open all year, first-come, first-serve; no trailers over 30 feet long

⟨ SERVICES | FACILITIES ⟩ None in park

⟨ NEARBY ACCOMMODATIONS | SERVICES ⟩ Lodging and full services in Bloomfield, Aztec, Farmington, Cuba, Grants, and Gallup, New Mexico

⟨ INFORMATION ⟩ Superintendent, Chaco Culture National Historical Park, P.O. Box 220, Nageezi, NM 87037; phone: 505-786-7014; website www.nps.gov/chcu

Chamizal National Memorial is a small park dedicated to a big idea— that two nations can coexist in friendship and peace.

Chamizal
NATIONAL MEMORIAL

Chamizal National Memorial is a small park dedicated to a big idea—that two nations can coexist in friendship and peace. The memorial was established in 1963 by a treaty between the United States and Mexico to settle a protracted, complex boundary dispute.

This fifty-five-acre green space and arts center in El Paso, Texas, sits beside the Rio Grande, or Rio Bravo as it's known in Mexico. Like many rivers, the Rio Grande has a will of its own. Through time, the river wandered across the wide alluvial plain at El Paso. In these channel changes, land was taken away from one country and given to the other. These pieces of land are called *bancos*. The Chamizal parcel, located just upstream of today's memorial, was a banco cut off from Mexico. The name Chamizal is Spanish for plants that grow beside the river— chamiza and carrizo.

In 1848 the international boundary was declared to be the deepest portion of the Rio Grande. But because of the river's propensities, this was a "living" boundary. As early as 1852, as surveyors tried to mark the precise line separating the two countries, the difficulties became apparent. An early opinion of the United States' attorney general said that if land shifted slowly as a result of erosion, the boundary moved with the river. But if the move was sudden due to flooding, the boundary was to remain in the original location. This complicated principle became entrenched as international law where rivers formed boundaries.

Both countries made claims and counterclaims to the Chamizal parcel. As El Paso and its sister city, Ciudad Juárez, Mexico, grew, the issue became more critical. Developers desired land, but clear ownership and title were needed before anyone would undertake development. In 1911, an arbitration process divided the Chamizal parcel along the 1864 riverbed. But that decision failed to settle the dispute, and relations between the neighboring countries became bitter. Chamizal symbolized deeper problems, until finally the presidents of both nations intervened.

Mexican President Adolfo López Mateos and United States President John F. Kennedy directed ambassadors Manuel Tello and Thomas C. Mann to address the matter. On August 29, 1963, the Chamizal treaty was signed. The men pressed their rings into warm crimson wax and sealed the treaty, which called for a transfer of land, relocation of nearly 5,000 residents, and confinement of the Rio Grande to a concrete channel to curtail its wanderings permanently. Both countries shared the costs of the settlement of the century-long dispute.

The formal transfer of land took place in 1967. Part of that included the creation of Chamizal National Memorial.

Above: Two nations' flags fly in partnership above Chamizal National Memorial.

The scenic eight-mile drive to Massai Point in Chiricahua National Monument puts you on top of the world.

and toads; 1 kind of turtle; and 700 flowering plants and ferns, not to mention innumerable insects and others of their ilk.

The distinct south-of-the-border flavor adds great diversity to the animal world. Birds such as sulphur-bellied flycatchers, elegant trogons, red-faced warblers, Mexican chickadees, and blue-throated and magnificent hummingbirds reach their northern limits here. A few people search the Chiricahuas for a very rare bird—the thick-billed parrot. The last reliable report of this tropical species in the United States came from Rhyolite Canyon in the Chiricahuas in 1938. The parrots were reintroduced into these mountains in the late 1980s and 1990s, but the final chapter is yet to be written on their success.

Plant communities range from mesquite grass-lands through chaparral and evergreen oaks, and into pine forest. There are thirteen species of pines and oaks here alone, including Apache and Chihuahua pines and Mexican and Emory oaks. Handsome Apache fox squirrels sprawl on the tree branches, while piglike javelinas and irresistible coatimundis snuffle among stream boulders.

This mountainous maze was an ideal hiding place for the Apache, the latest representatives of Native occupants who had lived in these lands for thousands of years. After decades of raids and counter raids among Apaches, Spaniards, and Anglo-Americans, the U.S. military was bent on routing out the last great warriors, including Cochise, Geronimo, Natchez, and Mangus. In 1886, with soldiers encamped in Bonita Canyon, General Nelson Miles rounded up Apaches and

Chiricahua
NATIONAL MONUMENT

The scenic eight-mile drive to Massai Point in Chiricahua National Monument puts you on top of the world. Stretching out before you is a con-voluted maze of statuesque rocks sculpted by water and ice over millions of years.

This part of southeast Arizona was born of fire. The source of it all was the Turkey Creek caldera ten miles to the south. The caldera (the word is Spanish for cauldron) formed when a bubble of magma domed up surface rock, then erupted along an encircling ring 25 million years ago. Fiery, gaseous, glowing clouds, called *nuée ardentes*, put on a fantastic show of pyrotechnics, a thousand times more powerful than the eruption of Mount Saint Helens.

Voluminous quantities of ash and volcanic sand were mixed with the gases. The material was so hot that it fused into layers called welded tuff. Continuing eruptions filled the caldera and spilled out over nearly 700 square miles of land. Geologists discern nine distinct layers, together forming the 880-foot-thick Rhyolite Canyon Formation.

The drive to Massai Point increases from just over 5,000 feet to more than 7,000 feet elevation. This range in elevation through the park's 12,000 acres—along with the geographical confluence of the Sonoran and Chihuahuan deserts and the close proximity of Mexico—make Chiricahua a biological paradise too. Numbers of species in each category in this relatively small area are impressive: 170 bird species; 70 types of mammals; an astound-ing 32 different kinds of snakes; 16 lizards; 9 frogs

Right: A thunderstorm forms behind Balanced Rock.

sent them to a reservation in Florida. Geronimo surrendered, but a few last holdouts, notably Big Foot Massai, escaped near what is now called Massai Point.

One of those Army soldiers was Swedish immigrant Neil Erickson, who married Emma Peterson. They ranched at the mouth of Bonita Canyon, and their two daughters, Lillian and Hildegard, stayed on the homestead and expanded their land holdings into what is known as the Faraway Ranch. Lillian married Ed Riggs, and together they worked to preserve the geologic and biologic wonder that is Chiricahua National Monument.

Below: Bonita Canyon in winter

CHIRICAHUA NATIONAL MONUMENT
VISITOR INFORMATION

❮ OPEN ❯ Year-round except Christmas Day

❮ VISITOR CENTER ❯ Open 8 a.m.–4:30 p.m. daily, closed Christmas; exhibits, books

❮ ENTRANCE FEE ❯ Yes

❮ CAMPING ❯: Bonita Canyon Campground; first-come, first-serve; tents and RVs 29 feet or less in length; additional camping in Coronado National Forest

❮ SCENIC DRIVES ❯ Bonita Canyon Scenic Drive, paved, 8 miles one way

❮ SERVICES | FACILITIES ❯ Restrooms, water, picnicking

❮ NEARBY ACCOMMODATIONS | SERVICES ❯ Gasoline, food, and lodging in Willcox, Arizona

❮ INFORMATION ❯ Superintendent, Chiricahua National Monument, 13063 E. Bonita Canyon Rd., Willcox, AZ 85643; phone: 520-824-3560; website: www.nps.gov/chir

. . .the long line of armored marchers forged inland, eventually traveling thousands of miles through what would become the American Southwest. . .

Coronado
NATIONAL MEMORIAL

On February 22, 1540, Francisco Vázquez de Coronado placed his hand on a missal and swore that as a good Christian he would use his position "to uphold the service of God and his Majesty, would obey and execute his commands. . . as a gentleman should do."

Coronado's position was captain general of an expedition into the northern frontier of New Spain. His primary goal was to locate the Seven Cities of Cíbola, alleged metropolises of gold. The day after taking his oath, the young Coronado set out from Compostela, Mexico, with some 400 soldiers, four priests, hundreds more Mexican-Indian allies and servants, and some 1,500 head of livestock. Over the next two years, the long line of armored marchers forged inland, eventually traveling thousands of miles through what would become the American Southwest and into the Great Plains. It was the first documented European exploration of this country, and in recognition of the expedition Coronado National Memorial was established.

Though Coronado did not actually set foot in the 4,750 acres of land in the memorial, he did pass just to the east, up the valley of the San Pedro River.

Coronado National Memorial sits at the south end of the rugged Huachuca Mountains, which rise to more than 9,000 feet. From the park, visitors have a full view of the verdant valley of the San Pedro River looping north from Mexico. Because the river still carries water, it is a veritable line of life for humans and many types of birds and other wildlife.

Golden grasslands and evergreen oaks grow in the foothills of the park, and the oaks become more numerous as elevation increases (the park contains some ten species of oaks alone). Higher still, Mexican piñons mix with massive alligator junipers. Spiky-leaved sotols and agaves punctuate the rocky hillsides, along with shrubs like silk tassel and sumac. This borderland country is also rich with species that reach northward from Mexico—insistent gray jays, unusual hummingbirds, endearing coatimundis, and diminutive Coues whitetail deer. Cooper's hawks nest in sycamores in Montezuma Canyon, while Mearn's quail skitter in the oak leaf litter. Other rare creatures, such as barking frogs and long-nosed bats, also find this a favorable environment.

Ranchers and homesteaders settled in the area in the late 1800s and early 1900s, and prospectors roamed the mountains looking for silver, copper, and gold. One of the longest running operations was the State of Texas Mine up in Montezuma Canyon. Mining engineer Tom Sparkes was one of the owners. When he died, his daughter Grace inherited his share. While helping run the mine, Grace Sparkes became entranced with the region's history and worked without rest to have a park set aside to commemorate the Coronado expedition. President Harry Truman designated the memorial in 1952.

Above: Montezuma Peak, the park's highest point, is 7,676 feet.

CORONADO NATIONAL MEMORIAL
VISITOR INFORMATION

‹ OPEN › Year-round dawn to dusk, closed Thanksgiving and Christmas days

‹ VISITOR CENTER › 9 a.m.–5 p.m. daily except Thanksgiving and Christmas; exhibits, video, books

‹ ENTRANCE FEE › No

‹ CAMPING › None; in nearby Coronado National Forest

‹ SERVICES | FACILITIES › Restrooms, drinking water, picnic area

‹ NEARBY ACCOMMODATIONS | SERVICES › Sierra Vista and Hereford, Arizona

‹ INFORMATION › Superintendent, Coronado National Memorial, 4101 E. Montezuma Canyon Rd., Hereford, AZ 85615; phone: 520-366-5515; website: www.nps.gov/coro

A boat trip on Morrow Point Reservoir, sequestered within Black Canyon's steep, dark walls, is a memorable experience.

A trio of reservoirs stairsteps down the Gunnison River in west-central Colorado to form Curecanti National Recreation Area. The reservoirs and surrounding lands are a big playground for everything from boating and fishing to windsurfing and wildlife watching.

Curecanti (the name is for Ute leader Curicata) is the product of a federal dam-building program in the 1960s and 1970s. Blue Mesa Dam was the first, constructed on the Gunnison River in 1965. The 342-foot-high dam forms Blue Mesa Reservoir, filling an open sagebrush basin. Blue Mesa was the first large dam on the Gunnison, and the 9,000-acre lake is the largest in the state of Colorado. Just downstream, the water enters the confines of Black Canyon. Here Morrow Point Reservoir was created by Morrow Point Dam,

Curecanti Needle, a landmark rock that the company adopted as the icon of its "Scenic Line of the World." At Cimarron, visitors can still see one of the helper engines, old 278, and walk a short stretch of the original bed on the Pine Creek Trail.

Crystal Reservoir, the last of the three, is another haven for small boats. Owners carry in their craft on the Mesa Creek Trail, exercising caution in the event of sudden water releases from Morrow Point Dam. Wildlife sightings on this secluded reservoir include waterfowl, bighorn sheep, and the elusive river otter.

Left: Morrow Point Reservoir, created by Morrow Point Dam in 1970

Curecanti
NATIONAL RECREATION AREA

finished in 1970. The last of the three, Crystal Reservoir, was formed by its namesake dam, built in 1976.

Curecanti's dams and reservoirs, operated by the Bureau of Reclamation, furnish hydroelectric power and water to western states.

While the water projects serve their utilitarian duty, visitors are afforded a long list of recreational pursuits. Around Blue Mesa, much of that activity has to do with fish. The big reservoir is stocked with rainbow trout and famed kokanee salmon. Lake trout and Mackinaw are also plentiful. Summer finds windsurfers taking advantage of the frequent breezy conditions out on the wide-open waters. Hikers and campers have access to many trails and campgrounds. Bird watchers find the loose-woven nests of a great blue heron rookery in the cottonwoods at the headwaters of the reservoir near Neversink.

In winter figure skaters and ice fishermen are attracted to the frozen reservoir, while cross-country skiers glide across snowy hills and mesas. Bald eagles flock here in winter, and the area also serves as critical winter range for deer, elk, and bighorn sheep.

Just below Blue Mesa is Black Canyon, whose metamorphic rock walls are close to two billion years old. A boat trip on Morrow Point Reservoir, sequestered within Black Canyon's steep, dark walls, is a memorable experience. Entry is along the Pine Creek Trail, via 232 steps, so private boaters carry in only small craft.

In the last century, passengers on the Denver & Rio Grande Railway knew they had entered Black Canyon when they spied the 700-foot-high

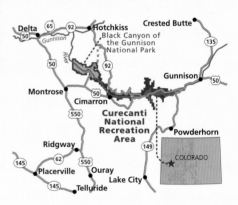

CURECANTI NATIONAL RECREATION AREA
VISITOR INFORMATION

《 OPEN 》 Year-round

《 VISITOR CENTERS 》 Elk Creek open 8 a.m.–4:30 p.m. in winter, extended hours the rest of the year; exhibits, books, interpretive programs; Cimarron open 9 a.m.–4 p.m. mid-May through September; Lake Fork 9 a.m.–4 p.m. mid-May through September; East Portal ranger station seasonally

《 ENTRANCE FEE 》 No, but fee for boat permit

《 CAMPING 》 Elk Creek open all year; three other developed campgrounds, Lake Fork, Stevens Creek, and Cimarron open seasonally; Dry Gulch, East Portal, Gateview, Ponderosa, and Red Creek open seasonally with various facilities; East Elk Creek and Red Creek group camps available by reservation; several boat-in campsites along all three reservoirs

《 SERVICES | FACILITIES 》 Groceries, boat rentals, guides, showers at Elk Creek and Lake Fork marinas; restaurant at Elk Creek in summer

《 NEARBY ACCOMMODATIONS | SERVICES 》 Gunnison, Sapinero, Cimarron, and Montrose, Colorado

《 INFORMATION 》 Superintendent, Curecanti National Recreation Area, 102 Elk Creek, Gunnison, CO 81230; phone: 970-641-2337; website: www.nps.gov/cure

Lava tubes, ice caves, sinkholes, spatter cones, pressure ridges, and craters are among the many attractions within the 590 square miles of tortured black lava.

El Malpais
NATIONAL MONUMENT AND CONSERVATION AREA

A three-mile loop trail in the El Calderon area provides visitors a good introduction to El Malpais. The first stop along the trail is at Junction Cave. Actually a lava tube, it formed in the same way as many other similar features in the park: exterior lava cooled and hardened, while still-molten liquid underneath continued moving out and beyond, leaving a vacant cavern inside.

The caves and lava tubes of El Malpais hold unique plants and animals. The entrances are festooned with green gardens of lichens and mosses. Canyon tree frogs inhabit crevices, along with the occasional gopher snake. An assortment of invertebrates—beetles, mites, camel crickets, spiders, springtails, and worms—inhabits the deeper, dark parts of the caves.

Lava tubes, ice caves, sinkholes, spatter cones, pressure ridges, and craters are among the many attractions within the 590 square miles of tortured black lava that stretch south of Grants, New Mexico, near the Continental Divide. Another cave, called Candelaria, which contains ice year-round, provided the initial impetus to set aside the area as some kind of park. In 1987, the federal government designated 114,000 acres as El Malpais National Monument and another 262,000 acres surrounding it as a national conservation area.

Geologists have mapped more than a dozen major lava flows in El Malpais, representing one of the longest sequences of volcanic eruptions in the country, from about a million to 3,000 years ago.

El Malpais—"bad country"—the early Spanish explorers called it. Most travelers circumvented the difficult terrain if they could, but Antonio de Espejo recorded crossing the "waterless malpais"

in 1582. In 1853, surveying for a railroad route along the 35th parallel, Lieutenant Amiel Weeks Whipple wrote: "The whole length of the valley followed today has been threaded by a sinuous stream of lava. It appears as if it had rolled down a viscous semi-fluid mass, had been arrested in its course, hardened, blackened, cracked, and in places broken."

While these Euro-Americans found the land forbidding, the people of neighboring Acoma and Zuni pueblos had been walking across the jagged terrain along a trade route for perhaps a thousand years. Visitors can still follow a portion of the Zuni-Acoma Trail today.

Despite the seemingly inhospitable terrain, El Malpais hosts an amazing variety of plants and wildlife. More than 70 species of mammals—from deer and elk to chipmunks, squirrels, prairie dogs, and pocket gophers—are known in the park. More than 100 species of birds have been recorded. And many reptiles can be seen, including eastern fence lizards, tree lizards, Great Plains skinks, short-horned lizards, prairie rattlesnakes, and gopher snakes. Several rare plants grow in specialized evironments.

Above: McCarty's lava flow with sandstone bluff

EL MALPAIS NATIONAL MONUMENT AND CONSERVATION AREA
VISITOR INFORMATION

❰ OPEN ❱ Year-round

❰ VISITOR CENTERS ❱ El Malpais Information Center (NPS) open 8:30 a.m.–4:30 daily except Thanksgiving, Christmas, and New Year's days; El Malpais Ranger Station (BLM) open 8:30 a.m.–4:30 p.m. daily except Thanksgiving, Christmas and New Year's

❰ ENTRANCE FEE ❱ No

❰ CAMPING ❱ No developed sites in national monument but backcountry, primitive camping allowed with permit. In the conservation area, five camping sites available in The Narrows picnic area

❰ SERVICES | FACILITIES ❱ Restrooms, water at information centers, picnic areas

❰ NEARBY ACCOMMODATIONS | SERVICES ❱ Grants, New Mexico

❰ INFORMATION ❱ Superintendent, El Malpais National Monument, 123 E. Roosevelt Ave., Grants, NM 87020; phone: 505-783-4774; website: www.nps.gov/elma; National Conservation Area, Bureau of Land Management, P.O. Box 846, Grants, NM 87020; phone: 505-280-2918.

Today El Morro is an archive, authentic and precious, that speaks volumes about historic events in the West.

El Morro
NATIONAL MONUMENT

A soft breeze rattles the slender cattails that line the quiet pool of water. Tidy mud nests of cliff swallows fit into tiny crevices above it. The shriek of a falcon echoes off the high sandstone walls.

First, nature varnished the cliff face of El Morro with coppery streamers. Then American Indians pecked symbols and images onto the stone as they came down from the mesa-top to fetch water at the pool. The first European-Americans to inscribe the rock were Spaniards. With elaborate penmanship they left their names and dates—often beginning with the words *paso por aqui*, "passed by here." Later inscriptions took on a more official tone, though a few were moved to poetry.

The cliff soars 200 feet above the woodland of western New Mexico, its buff-colored sandstone unmistakable and the pool of water at its base irresistible. For uncounted centuries El Morro stood as a landmark, a guidepost, and a guest register for travelers in the Southwest. Today El Morro is an archive, authentic and precious, that speaks volumes about historic events in the West.

To the Zuni, who now live in a pueblo nearby, this place is A'ts'ina. In the late 1200s, their ancestors lived in a huge pueblo on top of the high bluff. The village had been vacant for nearly 300 years when Don Juan de Oñate came through in 1605. He called it Aqua de la Pena, "water of the rock," but soon the Spaniards renamed it El Morro, "the headland," because that is what the bold formation resembled to their eyes. In English, it became simply Inscription Rock.

Walking along the Inscription Rock trail, visitors first come upon the pourover pool that furnished that life-saving substance in this dry land. Beyond, mostly at eye level on the flat rock face, are the inscriptions, some faint and worn, others as clear as if they'd been left last week. Here passed Miguel Alfaro, Ramon Jurado, Pedro Romero, Juan Archuleta, along with their more famous countrymen—Oñate in April of 1605 and General Don Diego de Vargas in 1692, the year he reconquered New Mexico. More Spaniards left their names, the last in 1774.

On September 17 and 18, 1849, the first English names were applied. Government explorers James H. Simpson and artist Richard Kern copied all the inscriptions on the rock and then left their own, complete with a corrected spelling error. In 1858, a wagon train of California-bound emigrants camped for the night by the pool, scratching their names onto the rock. One was 63-year-old John Udell, a Baptist preacher who with his wife and ragtag group had been forced to turn back from their intended destination. Civil War veterans and railroad surveyors stopped in the 1860s, the Union Pacific Railroad men leaving the initials "U.P.R."

When the main rail line went in just north of El Morro, the rock's service as a milepost for east-west travelers came to an end. Visitors today view this historical tablet, fortunate to know of people who once left word of their passage.

Above: Inscription Rock at sunrise

EL MORRO NATIONAL MONUMENT
VISITOR INFORMATION

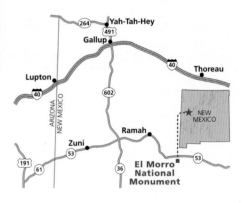

〈 OPEN 〉 Year-round except Christmas and New Year's days

〈 VISITOR CENTER 〉 Hours vary with season; call park for current times; museum, video, book sales

〈 ENTRANCE FEE 〉 Yes

〈 CAMPING 〉 Yes, nine sites suitable for tents and RVs less than 27 feet long, first-come, first-serve (no fee in winter, water turned off)

〈 SERVICES I FACILITIES 〉 Restrooms, water, picnic area

〈 NEARBY ACCOMMODATIONS I SERVICES 〉 Full services in Grants and Gallup, New Mexico, limited services at Zuni

〈 INFORMATION 〉 Superintendent, El Morro National Monument, HC61, Box 43, Ramah, NM 87321; phone: 505-783-4226; website: www.nps.gov/elmo

Apache camp, Indian agency, stage station, and Army post—Fort Bowie played all these roles at one time or another in its high-profile spot on the stage of Southwest history.

The site's importance is due to the existence of a flowing spring and a natural gateway through the mountains of southern Arizona. But between 1850 and 1880, this bucolic place was the site of violence and bloodshed.

The natural pass, or saddle, extends between the Dos Cabezas and Chiricahua Mountains, at 5,000 feet elevation. It is a land of oaks and mesquites amid volcanic and limestone rock. Native Southwesterners, first the Mogollon people and then the Apaches, took advantage of the area's richness and made homes here. They guarded the water source, Apache Spring, and lived on acorns,

Washington Bowie, was built that same year. It served only seven years before another one was erected a few hundred yards to the east.

Cochise accepted peace in 1872, while Geronimo, the last great Apache leader, surrendered in 1886. Geronimo and other leaders were briefly held at Fort Bowie before their removal from the Southwest.

With the Apache wars at an end, Fort Bowie's days were numbered. Finally, in 1894, the fort was closed for good, concluding a significant era in Southwest military affairs.

Visitors can still see partial adobe walls and rock foundations of many of the fort's buildings.

> The site's importance is due to the existence of a flowing spring and a natural gateway through the mountains of southern Arizona.

Fort Bowie
NATIONAL HISTORIC SITE

mesquite beans, cactus fruits, and the sweet hearts of agave.

To early Spaniards this was Puerto del Dado, Pass of Chance. Forty-niners on their way to the California gold fields traveled up Siphon Canyon to reach Apache Pass. They were greeted, sometimes with hostility, by the Chiricahua Apache led by Cochise.

In 1854 Lieutenant John Parke camped two days at Apache Pass, as he surveyed a railroad route along the 32nd parallel. Although the rails did not come this way, the stage lines did. In July 1858, the Butterfield Overland Mail began its 2,800-mile run from Tipton, Missouri, to San Francisco, stopping four times a week at the sturdy rock station at Apache Pass.

In 1861 relations worsened between the resident Indians and the newcomers. The encampment of Second Lieutenant George Bascom and his soldiers near the stage station precipitated a crisis. Bascom confronted Cochise over the kidnapping of a boy and theft of livestock. Cochise, falsely accused, escaped when he realized what awaited him.

A battle a year later, at the beginning of the Civil War, sparked the establishment of Fort Bowie. On July 15, 1862, Brigadier General James Carleton's Union troops, the California Volunteers, were marching east to engage the Confederates. Guarding the coveted spring at Apache Pass, Cochise and his warriors waited on the hill called Overlook Ridge. They took the soldiers by surprise with their fire, but the Union howitzers finally forced their retreat.

To secure the spring and the pass for travelers, the first fort, named for Colonel George

FORT BOWIE NATIONAL HISTORIC SITE
VISITOR INFORMATION

❮ OPEN ❯ Year-round. Fort and visitor center accessible on 1.5-mile foot trail. Handicapped call for directions to accessiblity road. Trailhead on Apache Pass Road south of Bowie, Arizona. Road slippery when wet, and subject to flash floods

❮ VISITOR CENTER ❯ Open 8 a.m.–4:30 p.m.; trail open sunrise to sunset; exhibits, books, ranger walks by special arrangement

❮ ENTRANCE FEE ❯ No

❮ CAMPING ❯ None; nearest in Coronado National Forest or Chiricahua National Monument

❮ SERVICES | FACILITIES ❯ Drinking water and restrooms

❮ NEARBY ACCOMMODATIONS | SERVICES ❯ Willcox and Bowie, Arizona

❮ INFORMATION ❯ Chief Ranger, P.O. Box 158, Bowie, AZ 85605; phone: 520-847-2500; website: www.nps.gov/fobo

Left: Partial adobe walls and rock foundations are all that remain of this western outpost.

were lined up, fifteen or so side by side, the last names marking their claims—Allen, Lynch, Dupree, Wallace, Rousey, Tripps, and Claggett.

The Buffalo Soldiers helped build the new Fort Davis, including Officers' Row, a line of gracious stone buildings with neat white columns, porches facing the parade ground. The officers' quarters had kitchens separate from the main structure, where a cook (often a woman) prepared meals for the resident officer. Beyond Officers' Row, the fort eventually grew to include eight barracks, a large commissary, several storehouses, corrals, a chapel, a bakery, and even a good-sized hospital. In the early 1880s, white troops joined the Buffalo Soldiers in garrisoning the post.

The only thing that introduced much variety into the otherwise monotonous life was

> Fort Davis's prime mission was to protect travelers and the mail along the San Antonio-El Paso Road out in the wild trans-Pecos region.

FORT DAVIS NATIONAL HISTORIC SITE
VISITOR INFORMATION

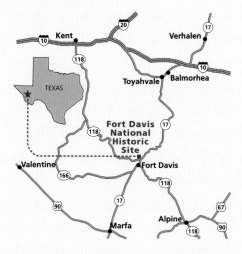

〈 OPEN 〉 Year-round, except Thanksgiving, Christmas, New Year's, and Martin Luther King days

〈 VISITOR CENTER 〉 Located in former enlisted men's barracks, open 8 a.m.–5 p.m.; booksales, exhibits, auditorium, video; "sound program" of 1875 Dress Retreat Parade played outside three times a day; bugle call heard across parade field throughout day

〈 ENTRANCE FEE 〉 Yes

〈 CAMPING 〉 No; at adjoining Davis Mountains State Park

〈 SERVICES | FACILITIES 〉 Restrooms, water, picnic area

〈 NEARBY ACCOMMODATIONS | SERVICES 〉 Town of Fort Davis, Texas

〈 INFORMATION 〉 Superintendent, Fort Davis National Historic Site, P.O. Box 1379, Lt. Flipper Drive, Fort Davis, TX 79734; phone: 432-426-3224; website: www.nps.gov/foda

Fort Davis
NATIONAL HISTORIC SITE

The clear waters of Limpia Creek were reason enough for the United States Army to build a fort in the Davis Mountains of west Texas. That, and perhaps the inviting sight of wild roses and cottonwood trees. More likely, though, the big draw was the plenitude of water, wood, and grass at the mouth of a box canyon, against sheltering volcanic rock.

This is the spot Brevet Major General Persifor Smith chose in 1854 for a fort that was named for Secretary of War Jefferson Davis. Fort Davis's prime mission was to protect travelers and the mail along the San Antonio-El Paso Road out in the wild trans-Pecos region. The threat, in the Army's eyes, was the presence of Apache, Comanche, and Kiowa, who also knew of those clear waters and who felt a bit threatened themselves.

The fort's first buildings of thatch and wood soon yielded to stouter stone and adobe. Federal troops abandoned the post at the start of the Civil War. Confederate soldiers held it for a brief time in 1861 and 1862, then the fort was left to ruin until 1867. It was then rebuilt, serving for the next twenty-four years as a major link in a series of frontier fortresses.

Through much of the rest of its life, Fort Davis was home to the famed Buffalo Soldiers. These African Americans—many of them freed slaves and Civil War veterans—headed west. They found that joining the Army was a fair way to make a living in a new land. A soldier enlisted for five years and received thirteen dollars a month for his service. In the squad rooms of the enlisted men's barracks, each man was assigned a single wood-slatted bed with a hay-stuffed mattress. The bunks

"detached" duty. Soldiers worked at the pinery in the Davis Mountains, strung miles of telegraph line, built roads, guarded waterholes, patrolled the rugged Mexican border, provided military escort, and on rare occasions engaged in skirmishes with Apaches. The most notable Indian campaign involved Warm Springs Apache leader Victorio, who remained defiant until 1880, when he was finally driven south and killed by Mexican soldiers. When off duty, the troops occupied the long hours by playing cards, music, baseball, and partaking in a few rowdier pursuits off-post.

With the end of the Indian Wars, Fort Davis had "outlived its usefulness" and was closed for good in June 1891. Since 1961 the National Park Service has administered the site, which includes more than two dozen restored buildings, several of which visitors can enter. This is one of the best-preserved forts in the Southwest.

Buffalo Soldiers helped to build Officers' Row.

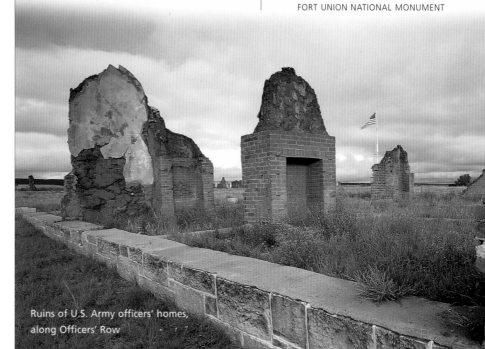

Ruins of U.S. Army officers' homes, along Officers' Row

In its day, Fort Union was a busy place full of sound and movement.

Fort Union
NATIONAL MONUMENT

FORT UNION NATIONAL MONUMENT
VISITOR INFORMATION

《 OPEN 》 Year-round except Thanksgiving, Christmas, and New Year's days

《 VISITOR CENTER 》 8 a.m.–6 p.m. Memorial Day to Labor Day; closes at 4 p.m. rest of year; park hours same; exhibits, booksales, information on special summer events

《 ENTRANCE FEE 》 Yes

《 CAMPING 》 None at site; nearest in Las Vegas and Raton, New Mexico, Storrie Lake State Park, and national forests

《 SERVICES | FACILITIES 》 Restrooms, water, picnic area

《 NEARBY ACCOMMODATIONS | SERVICES 》 Lodging, food, gasoline in Las Vegas, Raton, and Wagon Mound, New Mexico

《 INFORMATION 》 Superintendent, P.O. Box 127, Watrous, NM 87753; phone: 505-425-8025; website: www.nps.gov/foun

In a little more than a decade, from 1851 to 1863, three United States military forts were built out on the plains of northeast New Mexico to fend off Indians, fight Confederates, and protect travelers on the Santa Fe Trail. All three were called Fort Union, but it was the third and final fort that became the largest such establishment on the southwestern frontier.

Out on the quiet plains today, only the shell of the third fort remains—adobe walls and brick chimneys, remnants of the original flagstone path that stretched in front of Officers' Row, the small grim prison. But in its day, Fort Union was a busy place full of sound and movement. Walking the grounds, visitors can almost hear the creak and groan of wagon wheels over rocky ground, the crack of the bull whacker's whip coaxing the oxen on, the hustle and hoopla upon a wagon's arrival at the quartermaster depot, the ring of the blacksmith's hammer repairing axles and wheels, the sunrise bugle reveille competing with the warbles of meadowlarks in the fields, the braying of mules and snorting of horses in the post corral, the snap of salutes and click of heels when a new officer arrived.

The Santa Fe Trail was the main reason for the location of Fort Union. This 800-mile-long route of commerce from Missouri to Santa Fe was a two-month journey for wagons laden with several tons of goods. In use since 1821, the trail was vulnerable to attack by resident Indians. After 1846, when the United States took New Mexico as its own, the government decided to station troops out where the trail's Mountain Branch and Cimarron Cutoff converged.

So in July 1851, Colonel Edwin Vose Sumner arrived with his dragoons to erect the first Fort Union. Though hastily constructed of green logs that warped as they dried, it did serve for ten years. But by 1861, with the beginning of the Civil War, its poor state of repair led to abandonment. As the tour begins, visitors cross the faint ruts of the Santa Fe Trail and see the site of the First Fort out across the valley.

The second fort was built nearby to defend the Union against Confederate troops entering New Mexico along the Rio Grande. An earthwork construction in the shape of a four-cornered star, it is sometimes called the "Star Fort." The anticipated battle never took place at the fort— the Confederates were stopped at Glorieta Pass in March 1862. The Star Fort was a dank, unpleasant place, and in only two years plans again were under way to build a better post.

The third and last Fort Union was under construction in 1863. This time, it would become a large, livable facility consisting of a military post and quartermaster and ordnance depots. Stone, adobe, and clay bricks were obtained locally, while nails and glass came by way of the Santa Fe Trail.

When off duty, an enlisted man filled the hours with hunting, fishing, reading *Harper's Weekly* at the post library, engaging in a fierce baseball game, drinking, or gambling. On occasion, troops saw action when they went out to patrol the Santa Fe Trail and encountered the Comanche, Kiowa, Apache, or Navajo. But by 1875, even that threat was diminished. By 1879, with the arrival of the railroad into nearby Watrous, the Santa Fe Trail was destined to revert to two parallel tracks in the ground. Fort Union remained garrisoned until 1891, when it was finally closed.

Wall of Mechanics' Yard

In 1885 Army Lieutenant G. H. Sands, scouting in southern New Mexico, came upon stone dwellings high up in a cliff in the headwaters of the Gila River. He and his companion hoisted themselves up the steep slope and found a one-story house set in the face of the cliff. They could not get into it but pushed farther along the cliff face and found "quite a long line of houses. . .set like a nest in the face of the wall." The pair entered the rooms, which were joined by small doorways, and found sound wooden rafters, pieces of pottery, and arrowheads.

The dwellings are located in alcoves 180 feet above the floor of Cliff Dweller Canyon, a tributary of the Gila River. They are the reason Gila Cliff Dwellings National Monument was designated, and they are the only representative sites in the

The cliff dwellers abandoned their homes and fields by the early 1300s. Why they left and where they went are not known.

GILA CLIFF DWELLINGS NATIONAL MONUMENT
VISITOR INFORMATION

〈 OPEN 〉 Year-round, except Christmas

〈 VISITOR CENTER 〉 Open 8 a.m.–5 p.m. Memorial Day to Labor Day, 8 a.m.–4:30 p.m. rest of year, closed Christmas and New Year's days; exhibits, video, booksales

〈 CONTACT STATION 〉 At cliff dwelling trailhead, 8 a.m.–6 p.m. Memorial Day to Labor Day, 9 a.m.–4 p.m. in winter

〈 ENTRANCE FEE 〉 Yes

〈 CAMPING 〉 None on site; developed sites at upper and lower Scorpion Campgrounds 1/4 mile away; primitive camping at Forks and Grapevine campgrounds within six miles; dispersed camping possible throughout surrounding Gila National Forest and Gila Wilderness

〈 SERVICES | FACILITIES 〉 Water, restrooms, picnicking

〈 NEARBY ACCOMMODATIONS | SERVICES 〉 Gila Hot Springs and Silver City, New Mexico

〈 INFORMATION 〉 Superintendent, Gila Cliff Dwellings National Monument, HC 68, Box 100, Silver City, NM 88061; phone: 505-536-9461; website: www.nps.gov/gicl

Gila Cliff Dwellings
NATIONAL MONUMENT

national park system of the major southwestern culture known as the Mogollon.

In the late 1200s, the builders leveled the dirt floors, laid up mortared masonry walls using natural boulders in places, and plastered floors and walls inside the rooms. Hearths and pot rests indicate the rooms were used as living areas. Besides living rooms, there were also storage rooms, unroofed work spaces, and communal structures. All told there were about forty rooms, home to perhaps eight to ten families.

The Gila cliff dwellings bear a strong imprint of the ancestral Puebloans. Their location, construction methods, and signature T-shaped doorways are reminiscent of these northerners, who perhaps immigrated into the Mogollon territory or at least had strong influence here.

The residents enjoyed steady water from the creek and a permanent spring, farmland was available on the mesas and the river floodplain, and plants and animals were plentiful. Piñon pine, with a rich edible nut, would have been most valuable. In the foothills and valleys grew walnut, oak, grape, box elder, and yucca; mule deer, bison, turkeys, marmots, muskrats, and waterfowl provided additional food sources. The growing season at 6,000 feet averages 140 days, long enough to raise corn, beans, squash, and possibly amaranth and tobacco as well.

Timbers in the houses have produced tree-ring dates ranging from 1276 to 1287. Yet despite the time and energy devoted to building these dwellings, the people lived in them for only a generation. The cliff dwellers abandoned their homes and fields by the early 1300s. Why they left

and where they went are not known. Perhaps they joined other Pueblo people to the north or south.

Adolph Bandelier, whose name was given to archeological sites in northern New Mexico, wrote one of the earliest scientific descriptions of the Gila dwellings in 1884. He arrived when this rugged land was Apache territory.

After their rediscovery, the Gila dwellings were thoroughly pothunted. With pressure from archeological circles, President Theodore Roosevelt declared a 160-acre national monument in 1907, later enlarged to the present 533 acres.

Left: The Gila Cliff Dwellings are one of more than a hundred Mogollon sites throughout the Gila headwaters region.

The lake's surreal turquoise waters mirror a backdrop of red sandstone cliffs and dry benches and buttes.

Glen Canyon
NATIONAL RECREATION AREA

The gates of Glen Canyon Dam closed in 1963, the 710-foot-high arch of solid concrete holding back the waters of the Colorado River where it crosses from southern Utah into northern Arizona. Lake Powell, the reservoir that began filling behind the dam, would eventually extend 186 miles up-stream on the Colorado River. At 23 million acre-feet, Lake Powell is the second largest artificial lake in the nation, exceeded only by Lake Mead downstream. Glen Canyon Dam stores water and generates hydroelectric power for the Southwest.

Lake Powell is the centerpiece of Glen Canyon National Recreation Area, created in 1972. The lake's surreal turquoise waters mirror a back-drop of red sandstone cliffs and dry benches and buttes. Now, more than three million people a year come to boat, water ski, fish, hike, and camp. The nearly 2,000 miles of shoreline and almost a hun-dred side canyons offer as many opportunities on land as on water. A million acres of slickrock slot canyons and high broad mesas, including parts of the inspiring Escalante River drainage and the Kaiparowitz Plateau, await hardier explorers.

The lake is named for geologist John Wesley Powell, who navigated the length of the Green and Colorado rivers on an epic trip in 1869. It was Powell who bestowed the name Glen Canyon to this 200-mile stretch of the Colorado. He wrote of "royal arches, mossy alcoves, beautiful glens, and painted grottos," as well as vast chambers of carved rock soaring a thousand feet up to narrow lenses of sky.

Few ever saw these wonders before the waters of Lake Powell filled Glen Canyon, which then became "the place no one knew." Today, visitors launch houseboats, motorboats, sailboats, and kayaks at the marinas and head up- or downlake, mooring in quiet bays, swimming and relaxing under brilliant desert skies. In ever-narrowing side canyons where the lake waters stop, there is a totally different world of flowing streams with scoured pools shaded by redbud and cottonwood.

Scientists have combed the region for signs of earlier occupation. In the sediments of dry alcoves, paleontologists have unearthed the remains of ice-age mammals such as mammoths and ground sloths. Hot on the heels of the big mam-mals came roving hunter-gatherer folk. About 2,000 years ago, they began to stay put. These Basketmaker people left campsites in the Glen Canyon region. Later, the ancestral Puebloans built dwellings, made pottery, and etched designs and figures onto the rocks. They finally left the area around A.D. 1300.

In October 1776, two intrepid Spanish priests searched desperately for a way across the Colorado River. Fathers Domínguez and Escalante were hungry and hurrying to outrun winter. The place where they finally forded the river, the Crossing of the Fathers, is now hundreds of feet under the lake's Padre Bay. A handful of prospectors and rail-road surveyors came through in the last decades of the nineteenth century, along with Mormon colonists Charles Hall, Cass Hite, and John D. Lee, who operated ferries on the Colorado. Their names live on at Halls Crossing, Hite, and Lees Ferry.

Elevation in the recreation area varies between 3,000 to more than 7,000 feet; most of it is desert. Resident plants and animals are well adapted to the sparse rainfall, hot summer temperatures, and sometimes bone-numbing winter cold. Cacti, yucca, Mormon tea, blackbrush, and ricegrass hold onto rocky soils, with juniper and piñon trees at higher elevations. Rangy jackrabbits and coyotes survive well, along with packrats, pocket mice, and other small rodents that make up the backbone of the ecosystem. Somber cormorants and stately egrets stay close to shore, ravens and turkey vultures roost in alcoves, and canyon wrens call from secret hideouts. In the lake waters, exotic game fish, including coveted striped bass, have assumed dominance.

Above Right: The Colorado River at Horseshoe Bend
Above Left: Glen Canyon Dam

GLEN CANYON NATIONAL RECREATION AREA
VISITOR INFORMATION

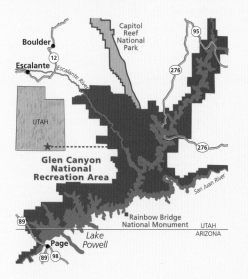

《 OPEN 》 Year-round

《 VISITOR CENTERS 》 Carl Hayden Visitor Center at Glen Canyon Dam open 8 a.m.–6 p.m. May through September, 8 a.m.–5 p.m. rest of year; exhibits, film, booksales; dam tours every half hour in summer, less frequently in winter

Bullfrog Visitor Center open 8 a.m.–5 p.m. April through October, intermittently in March, closed November through February; exhibits, booksales

Navajo Bridge Interpretive Center, open 9 a.m.–5 p.m. April through October; exhibits and books

Ranger stations: Halls Crossing, Hans Flat, Hite, Lees Ferry, Wahweap

《 ENTRANCE FEE 》 Yes

《 CAMPING 》 Developed campgrounds at Wahweap, Bullfrog, and Halls Crossing, RVs and tents; primitive campgrounds at Bullfrog, Hite, Lees Ferry, Lone Rock. Camping also allowed along the shore of Lake Powell outside developed areas (no facilities—must have own portable toilet or facilities on board boat)

《 LODGING | RESTAURANTS 》 Wahweap and Bullfrog. For information and reservations, call 800-528-6154

《 BOAT TOURS AND RENTALS 》 Concession-operated, phone 800-528-6154

《 NEARBY ACCOMMODATIONS | SERVICES 》 Page, Arizona

《 INFORMATION 》 Superintendent, Glen Canyon National Recreation Area, P.O. Box 1507, Page, AZ 86040; phone: 928-608-6404; website: www.nps.gov/glca

Top: Padre Bay and Gunsight Butte on Lake Powell
Above: The Escalante River at the Golden Cathedral

The Grand Canyon puts time—and our short lives—in perspective. It demands contemplation; it cannot be seen in a day, a week, or even a lifetime.

Most people's first view of the Grand Canyon is an astonishing experience. Staring into the abyss from a viewpoint on the rim, visitors often are left awed and speechless. What they mostly see is unending space filled with air and light, with a rock backdrop that hardly looks real.

At the deepest part of the gorge is a distant, small "V" of water. It is the Colorado River, the agent responsible for carving out this monumental space. This is not a cause that initially comes to mind. Surely something bigger or more catastrophic committed this act—earthquakes perhaps, or glaciers. Yet the Colorado was the abrasive conveyor belt that cut the canyon a mile deep and carried tons of debris to the ocean. Meanwhile, side-streams have eaten back into the rim to widen the canyon up to ten miles across, as the raven flies.

Surely such an achievement took a long time. It did in human terms, but not in geologic time. Best estimates have the Colorado chiseling the Grand Canyon to its present depth in only four million years, perhaps even as little as two million, a heartbeat in geologic time. The rocks that have been revealed, however, are much older than the canyon itself. In fact, the oldest rock here—the black, polished Vishnu Schist of the inner gorge—approaches two billion years old. Everything resting on top of the Vishnu is younger—the tan Tapeats Sandstone, the impenetrable Redwall, the crossbedded Coconino, to the rimrock Kaibab Limestone that clocks in at around 240 million years. This display represents one of the fullest exposures of rock in the world, a stony diary of the comings and goings of entire oceans, beaches,

Grand Canyon
NATIONAL PARK

Above: Crimson monkeyflower and box elder grow along Havasu Creek.
Right: View from Hopi Point, South Rim

rivers, mudflats, swamps, and deserts.

And so the Grand Canyon puts time—and our short lives—in perspective. It demands contemplation; it cannot be seen in a day, a week, or even a lifetime. And everyone has a unique reaction.

Most Grand Canyon visitors start on the South Rim. A number of viewpoints afford different, and equally fine, looks at the canyon. The Hermit Road out to the west passes Trailview, Powell, Pima, and Mojave points, to the last stop, Hermit's Rest. The "hermit" was Canadian-born Louis Boucher, who prospected and hosted tourists at his camps in Hermit and Boucher canyons.

Out on the East Rim, a stop at Grandview Point provides sights of other temples and buttes—Vishnu, Brahma, Zoroaster, Wotan's— names bestowed by geologist Clarence Dutton in the late nineteenth century.

Dutton was a contemporary of Major John Wesley Powell, the man credited as the first to navigate the Colorado River through Grand Canyon. During his 1869 expedition, Powell became the first to document the canyon's fantastic

geology, the first to map, measure, and apply Anglo-American names to its topographic features. Now, some 23,000 people a year see the canyon by boat on the Colorado. The roiling rapids and serene side canyons permit intimate views of the canyon's walls, waterfalls, tree frogs, and crimson monkeyflowers.

The North Rim provides yet another perspective. Averaging 8,000 feet in elevation, the North Rim stands a thousand feet higher than the South. The emerald forest of spruce and fir and aspen, and the canyon's more dissected, complex topography make a trip there highly worthwhile. The rare Kaibab squirrel, big grassy meadows, and petite sinkhole lakes add interest.

To begin to know the canyon itself, a walk below the rims is necessary. Even a short stroll down a trail reveals the profound silence, the sheer immensity, the particular details. It also highlights the extreme contrasts in environments. It's a desert down there, with temperatures 10 to 20 degrees warmer than the rims; water is a scarce commodity at most times of year. Longer hikes should be

tackled only with adequate preparation for what is always a rigorous endeavor. Canyon hiking takes a toll on knees and toes during the descent, and demands much physical stamina for the long, steep, ascent back out. But long after the pain is gone, the extraordinary canyon will stay in mind and heart.

Opposite Clockwise: View from Mather Point in winter, the Colorado River in Marble Canyon, and Havasu Creek at Havasu Canyon

GRAND CANYON NATIONAL PARK
VISITOR INFORMATION

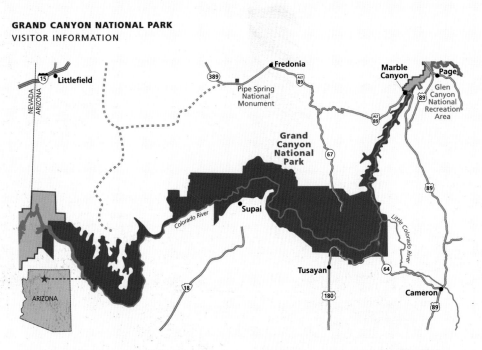

《 OPEN 》 South Rim open year-round, North Rim open mid-May to mid-October

《 VISITOR CENTERS 》 South Rim: Canyon View Information Plaza, open year-round 8 a.m.– 5 p.m., reachable by shuttle bus or short walk from Mather Point; Desert View Information Center at park's east entrance open year-round 9 a.m.–5 p.m., as staffing permits

North Rim: North Rim Visitor Center, open 8 a.m.–6 p.m. mid-May through mid-October; exhibits, book sales at each

《 PUBLIC TRANSPORTATION 》 A free shuttle-bus system operates year-round on the South Rim through Grand Canyon Village, to the South Kaibab Trailhead, and along Hermit Road

from March through November. North Rim reachable by private vehicle, until snow closes entrance road

《 ENTRANCE FEE 》 Yes

《 CAMPING 》 South Rim: Mather Campground open year-round, first-come, first-serve from December through March, by reservation from April through November, call 800-365-CAMP; Trailer Village with RV sites and hookups, call 888-297-2757 for information; Desert View Campground, open mid-May through mid-October, first-come, first-serve, tents and RVs (no hookups)

North Rim: North Rim Campground open mid-May to mid-October (no hookups). To reserve,

call 800-365-CAMP. After mid-October, limited primitive campsites available on first-come, first-serve basis, as long as road into park remains open.

Other camping available in adjoining Kaibab National Forest and in commercial campgrounds in nearby towns.

Phantom Ranch: Dormitory accommodations and meals at bottom of canyon for hikers and mule riders, operated by concessioner. Call 888-297-2757.

Backcountry Use: All backcountry camping and overnight uses require a permit from the Backcountry Information Center. Phone: 928-638-7875 (answered only from 1–5 p.m. Monday through Friday). Applications by mail or fax accepted 4 months in advance and recommended because of high demand for permits. Walk-in permits sometimes available for same day.

《 SERVICES I FACILITIES 》 Food, supplies, bank, and post office on South Rim; small camper store and gift shop on North Rim.

《 LODGING 》 Various motels and hotels on South Rim; Grand Canyon Lodge on North Rim. All lodging in park handled by Xanterra Parks & Resorts, call 888-297-2757

《 NEARBY ACCOMMODATIONS I SERVICES 》 Full services in Tusayan, Flagstaff, and Jacob Lake, Arizona

《 INFORMATION 》 Superintendent, Grand Canyon National Park, P.O. Box 129, Grand Canyon, AZ 86023; phone: 928-638-7888 (recorded message); website: www.nps.gov/grca

The sand dunes would not exist as they do without the surrounding Rocky Mountain environment.

Great Sand Dunes, the tallest dunes in North America, stand as elegant testament to the work of wind. The wind, plus uncountable grains of sand and a happy circumstance of topography, explains their existence in south-central Colorado.

The dune field covers 30 square miles, at least five billion cubic yards of palomino-colored sand piled more than 800 feet thick in the San Luis Valley. It all started with glacial debris washed out of the San Juan Mountains to the west and down into the valley, possibly 12,000 or more years ago. The dry lakes and silt left behind were blown by prevailing southwest winds into a pocket at the base of the Sangre de Cristo Mountains. That initial deposition is regularly refurbished by a grand-scale recycling process. Wind picks up the sand grains again, pushing them up toward the mountain passes.

But the wind loses strength and the sand drops out there. Reverse winds from the northeast then blow the sand back down toward the valley.

Medano and Sand creeks, draining off the Sangre de Cristos, play a critical role in the recycling process. They carry sand downstream, which is then blown back up against the mountains. Medano Creek, enclosing the eastern edge of the dunefield, exhibits an unusual phenomenon called surge, or pulsating, flow. As swift, shallow water flows down its smooth channel, sand ridges accumulate on the streambed. They build up until water pressure collapses them, accompanied by a pulse, or surge, of breaking waves.

Within this complex dunefield are found all the basic types of dunes—horn-shaped barchan dunes, transverse dunes, and reversing and star dunes, the highest in the park. It's tempting to walk barefoot out onto their sugary surfaces, but sand temperatures can reach a blistering 140 degrees Fahrenheit in summer.

A select few plants and animals have evolved to survive in this ever-shifting environment. Sprigs of green scurf pea, tendrils of blowout grass, and

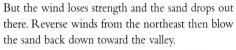

Great Sand Dunes
NATIONAL PARK AND PRESERVE

The park's ecosystem includes riparian, dune, and mountain areas.

Cottonwoods along Medano Creek

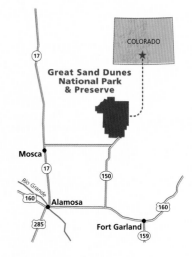

COLORADO

Great Sand Dunes National Park & Preserve

Mosca

Rio Grande

Alamosa

Fort Garland

❰ OPEN ❱ Year-round

❰ VISITOR CENTER ❱ Open 9 a.m.–6 p.m. Memorial Day to Labor Day; shorter hours in winter; closed some winter holidays; exhibits, video, books

❰ ENTRANCE FEE ❱ Yes

❰ CAMPING ❱ Piñon Flats Campground, first-come, first-serve, tents and smaller RVs, no hookups; designated car camping sites along Medano Pass Primitive Road (requires high clearance, 4WD vehicle); backcountry camping with free permit available at visitor center; additional camping in adjacent San Isabel National Forest

❰ SERVICES | FACILITIES ❱ Restrooms, water

❰ NEARBY ACCOMMODATIONS | SERVICES ❱ Great Sand Dunes Oasis just outside park has camping, lodge, restaurant, groceries, gasoline, showers, 4WD tours; full services in Alamosa, Colorado

❰ INFORMATION ❱ Superintendent, Great Sand Dunes National Park and Preserve, 11999 Highway 150, Mosca, CO 81146; phone: 719-378-6300; website: www.nps.gov/grsa

tawny Indian ricegrass weave among the dunes. In late summer in wet years, a massive bloom of prairie sunflowers gilds the sandy hummocks. Insects are the most common animal inhabitants on the dunes themselves. Seven species of beetles—including the gorgeous Great Sand Dunes tiger beetle and circus and clown beetles—are found only in and near these dunes. Kangaroo rats, which can metabolize all the water they need from the seeds they eat, are about the only mammals that live in the dunes. Tracks of others—coyote, bobcat, and mule deer—may be all one sees of their brief passage through the dunes.

The sand dunes would not exist as they do without the surrounding Rocky Mountain environment. With elevations ranging from 8,000 to more than 13,000 feet, the park encompasses everything from desert to tundra. The high desert of the San Luis Valley supports yucca, rabbitbrush, prickly pear, and blue grama grass. Underlying the valley is an important aquifer—groundwater that is being tapped at a rate that may not be sustainable by natural recharge. Wetlands occur in places. Although some hold surface water only part of the time, frogs and salamanders find homes in them.

East of the dunes, in the foothills of the Sangre de Cristos, piñon pine and Rocky Mountain juniper associate together in a woodland. The trees are not tall but can achieve great longevity. Every few years, piñons produce bumper crops of a rich, tasty nut that is both an important food to birds and squirrels and was a significant source of calories for Native people. Glorious old yellow-bellied ponderosa pines mix with the piñons. For the Ute, the sweet inner bark of ponderosa was survival food and medicine. Clutches of white-barked aspen lend a patchwork of color to the mountain landscape. Elk, bighorn, black bear, and mountain lion roam the deep forest and rocky breaks.

At even higher elevations, snow falls from November through April, lending silent beauty to forests of old-growth white fir and blue spruce. Limber pines and stunted bristlecone pines edge the treeline. Above this, on the highest peaks, exists the miniature world of alpine tundra, where plants hug the ground to avoid the chilling winds present any time of year. Here too are the headwater lakes of Medano and Sand creeks, fed by snowmelt. The creeks flow down through glacial-carved valleys brimming with wildflowers in summer, past narrowleaf cottonwoods gnawed by beavers, to the tawny desert grasslands where they cradle the famed dunes.

All this startling diversity is part of Great Sand Dunes National Park and Preserve.

Above: Rocky Mountain beeplant can grow at the edge of the dunes.

Still the question remains—
why would farming folk
undertake the building
of these impressive towers
at the very edges of
the canyons?

HOVENWEEP NATIONAL MONUMENT
VISITOR INFORMATION

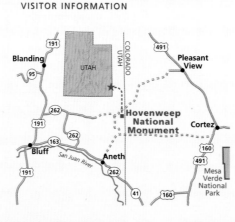

《 OPEN 》 Year-round

《 VISITOR CENTER 》 8 a.m.–5 p.m. daily, closed Thanksgiving, Christmas, and New Year's days; exhibits, books, audio-visual program; check for schedule of interpretive walks and talks and evening programs

《 ENTRANCE FEE 》 Yes

《 CAMPING 》 Yes, tents and RVs less than 25 feet long, no hookups; first-come, first-serve

《 SERVICES | FACILITIES 》 Restrooms, water, picnic area

《 NEARBY ACCOMMODATIONS | SERVICES 》 Cortez, Colorado, and Blanding, Utah

《 INFORMATION 》 Superintendent, Hovenweep National Monument, McElmo Route, Cortez, CO 81321; phone: 970-562-4282; website: www.nps.gov/hove

Hovenweep
NATIONAL MONUMENT

The word "Hovenweep" in the Ute/Paiute language means deserted valley. This valley was mostly deserted when explorers first saw and named it in the nineteenth century and remains sparsely inhabited today. Nature, rather than humans, holds sway here. A lizard darts silently across the path, the wind sighs in the piñon and juniper trees, and the sweet scent of cliffrose overwhelms the air.

But it was not always so. Seven hundred to 800 years ago, on the Great Sage Plain that sprawls across the boundary of Utah and Colorado, a few thousand people lived in thriving communities. They were ancestors of today's Pueblo Indians, and they chose this region to build some of the most enigmatic structures in the Southwest. They are stunning stone towers, located mostly at the heads of canyons with flowing springs. Hovenweep was designated a national monument in 1923 to preserve the remains of these towers with "the finest prehistoric masonry in the United States."

Ancestral Puebloans built most of the towers of Hovenweep in the mid 1200s. They first constructed round or square towers, while later ones such as Hovenweep Castle and Twin Towers were built in oval and D shapes. The builders laid up worked stones, in double and triple courses in some towers. These intriguing structures were a later manifestation of ancestral Puebloan architecture—wood in Hovenweep Castle produced a tree-ring date of A.D. 1277, making it one of the last Puebloan structures built in the San Juan River basin.

Along with the towers, they built pueblos and ceremonial rooms that formed communities. Checkdams, farming terraces, and granaries attest that dryland agriculture was also carried out at this prime 5,000-foot elevation. Corn, beans, squash, and amaranth were the main cultivated crops, but the Puebloans also possessed thorough knowledge of the uses of native plants such as serviceberry, sagebrush, and sumac.

Still the question remains—why would farming folk undertake the building of these impressive towers at the very edges of the canyons? Theories abound among archeologists. Various towers appear to have been places for living, working, and ceremony, as evidenced by the pottery, stone tools, and firepits found in them. Towers could have provided storage for surplus crops. Others may have been positioned to allow observations of solstices and equinoxes, important seasonal events for farmers. Researchers even went so far as to stand at the tops with lighted torches, exhibiting a possible signaling network from one tower to another. Certainly the canyon-framed view of Sleeping Ute Mountain could be reason enough to explain the towers' locations if not their use. Yet another interpretation comes from Rina Swentzell, a resident of Santa Clara Pueblo in New Mexico. She says that "people remained for awhile at Hovenweep creating the dark, interior spaces of the towers to balance the bright, strong, bouncing light of the canyon tops. . . ."

Beyond the Square Tower complex, Hovenweep also includes five outlying sites within about twenty miles. The Holly, Horseshoe, and Hackberry groups are closest, a few miles to the northeast in Colorado. Cutthroat Castle is about ten miles from Square Tower to the northeast, while the Cajon site is located an equal distance to the southwest in

Utah. Each of these sites also displays unique towers.

After nearly eight centuries, Hovenweep still possesses a strong mystique. Though we may never know for sure how the towers functioned, they will always display the remarkable skill and aesthetic sense of those who built them.

Above: Great House and Boulder House, Holly Ruins

Though the barter system was in force in most of the exchanges, Hubbell's and other posts used a form of currency called "tin money," accepted only at the posts where it was given.

Hubbell Trading Post
NATIONAL HISTORIC SITE

HUBBELL TRADING POST NATIONAL HISTORIC SITE
VISITOR INFORMATION

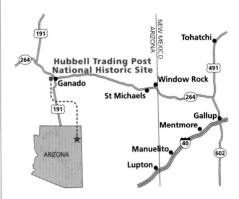

‹ OPEN › 8 a.m.–6 p.m. daily in summer; 8 a.m.–5 p.m. in winter; closed Thanksgiving, Christmas, and New Year's. Hubbell Trading Post is located on the Navajo Nation, which observes Daylight Saving Time; rest of Arizona on Mountain Standard Time, one hour behind the Navajo Nation from April through October.

‹ VISITOR CENTER › Same as park hours; exhibits, books, weaving demonstration; American Indian arts and crafts sold in trading post

‹ ENTRANCE FEE › No

‹ CAMPING › None

‹ SERVICES | FACILITIES › Restrooms, water, picnicking, snack foods at trading post

‹ NEARBY ACCOMMODATIONS | SERVICES › Chinle, Window Rock, and Chambers, Arizona

‹ INFORMATION › Superintendent, Hubbell Trading Post National Historic Site, P.O. Box 150, Ganado, AZ 86505; phone: 928-755-3475; website: www.nps.gov/hutr

In far eastern Arizona, under arching cottonwoods along Pueblo Colorado Wash, stands the oldest continuously operating trading post in the Navajo Nation. Hubbell Trading Post was established here in the 1870s, when Navajos resumed their lives after a bleak four-year exile at Fort Sumner in New Mexico.

John Lorenzo Hubbell went to work at the Navajo Agency at Fort Defiance in 1874. Two years later he was trading at Pueblo Colorado, and in 1878 purchased the store there from William Leonard. With partner C.N. Cotton, or with his own sons, Hubbell at various times had interests in more than thirty trading operations around the Navajo Nation and beyond in southern California. By this time Hubbell was known far and wide as "Don" Lorenzo, a Spanish title of honor. To the Navajo, his wire-rim glasses earned him the name Nák'ee Sinilí, "Eyeglasses."

While the Navajo had been trading sheep wool, blankets, and piñon nuts for years, with the advent of trading posts such as Hubbell's that commerce expanded. A much wider range of goods was available—Arbuckle coffee, canned fruit, fabrics, tools, and tobacco—and the Navajo were bringing in more wool, sheep, rugs, and jewelry in trade. Though the barter system was in force in most of the exchanges, Hubbell's and other posts used a form of currency called "tin money," accepted only at the posts where it was given.

After 1880, with the arrival of the Atlantic & Pacific railroad south of Pueblo Colorado, goods previously freighted by wagon went to the railhead for much speedier transport to the East.

Trading posts, and individual traders, served many functions. They sometimes housed and fed their customers, furnished important ceremonial items, accepted silver and turquoise jewelry as "pawn" for loans, hired local people, gave legal help, and occasionally even rendered medical assistance. John Lorenzo Hubbell was highly influential in shaping the products of weavers and silversmiths to market demands. He also enjoyed strong relationships with many Navajo, befriending clan leader Ganado Mucho, his son, and others.

In 1883 a stone building was put up, what is now the post's office and rug room. A few years later, as business grew, a larger wareroom was added. Beside the post was a farm that yielded fruits, vegetables, and alfalfa; a blacksmith shop; and a stout stone barn. The five-bedroom Hubbell family home, of thick adobe and heavy wood vigas, was well appointed with Navajo rugs, woven baskets, and a substantial art collection. A full-time baker turned out 400 loaves of bread a week to feed all the residents and guests.

John Lorenzo Hubbell died in 1930 and lies in the family cemetery on Hubbell Hill overlooking his first trading post. Beside him are his wife Lina, three of their children, and his dear Navajo friend, Many Horses. Hubbell's daughter-in-law, Dorothy, lived at the home until 1967, when it was turned over to the National Park Service.

Above: The post's "bullpen"
Right: The Hubbell dining room

In 1935 the 726-foot-high-dam was finished. Franklin D. Roosevelt stood on the crest and declared it "an engineering victory of the first order."

All this modern development took place in an old land. The rock of the stark hills, mountains, and canyons ranges from more than a billion to less than 5 million years in age. Located at the boundary between the Colorado Plateau and the Basin and Range provinces, these rocks record the passings of oceans, deserts, rivers, volcanoes, and sundering faults. The most recent period of extreme stretching of earth's crust twisted and torqued the flamboyantly tinted terrain in remarkable ways. It's a complex geologic story, some of which can be discovered by a drive along Lake Mead's Northshore Road.

Though elevations range from about 500 to more than 7,000 feet, most of the recreation area is desert, averaging only five inches of rain a year and summer temperatures hovering near 110 degrees Fahrenheit. Three major North American deserts touch here—the Sonoran, Mojave, and Great Basin—permitting a diverse array of plants and animals that exhibit successful adaptations. Desert tortoises, for example, store water beneath their hard shells, and adults can go a year without drinking. A healthy population of desert bighorn sheep thrives in the park, beautiful animals superbly suited to this dry, rocky terrain. Among plants, Joshua trees stand stiff and humanlike, drawing on moisture held in their stems and roots. Creosote bushes, which cover the valleys in olive green, have resin-impregnated leaves that give up little water; individual creosote bushes are known to survive for thousands of years. Wildflower seeds stay dormant in the soil until favorable winter and spring rains encourage their germination. In some years, the desert transforms into a garden of yellow poppies, sundrops, evening primroses, and phacelias.

Where water bubbles up from underground, as at Rogers and Blue Point springs, small splotches of shocking green exist—cattails, rushes, arrow-weed, and desert willow. These precious springs were likely well-known by early Native people

Lake Mead
NATIONAL RECREATION AREA

Like a watery dragon, Lake Mead twists along the border between Arizona and Nevada. Historic Hoover Dam forms Lake Mead, while below the dam Lake Mohave separates Arizona and California. Together the two reservoirs and surrounding land form 1.5-million-acre Lake Mead National Recreation Area. More than eight million people flock to the recreation area each year, boating, fishing, and swimming in the waters, and camping, driving, and walking amid the wild desert terrain.

When Hoover Dam was built in the 1930s, the nation was mired in the Great Depression. This ambitious public works project, the largest of its time, put thousands of men to work. To build the dam, the Colorado River was diverted from its course. Over the next three years, 4.5 million cubic feet of concrete was poured. In 1935 the 726-foot-high-dam was finished. Franklin D. Roosevelt stood on the crest and declared it "an engineering victory of the first order." The dam is a marvel of design and construction, and the story of the labor it demanded is another victory of sorts.

The lake created by Hoover Dam was named for U.S. Reclamation Commissioner Elwood Mead, and is the nation's largest artificial reservoir. Lake Mead supplies water to Nevada, Arizona, California, and Mexico, while the dam's turbines generate electricity for states all over the West. Lake Mohave came later, with the completion of Davis Dam in 1953. Lake Mead National Recreation Area was designated in 1964, the nation's first national recreation area.

Right: Iceberg Ridge (aerial)

who were in this desert 10,000 years ago. Actual signs of their presence in the recreation area, however, date back to about 5,000 years. The plants, animals, and other resources sheltered and fed them. By A.D. 1000, they were growing crops and building adobe structures such as those found at "Lost City," or Pueblo Grande de Nevada, on the Overton Arm of Lake Mead.

After earlier inhabitants left "Lost City," the Southern Paiute arrived, moving between the lower deserts and the higher country as the seasons changed. The Hualapai and Havasupai claimed lands in the western Grand Canyon region, while the Mojave lived on the lower Colorado.

In 1826, mountain man Jedediah Smith followed the Virgin River to its confluence with the Colorado, exploring salt deposits along the way. Miners and prospectors passed through, and in the 1850s paddlewheel steamboats chugged up the Colorado. Mormon settlers established small communities and ran ferries across the river, and their presence is marked at places on Lake Mead like Callville and Pearce Ferry.

Geologists think the Colorado River has

flowed through what is now Lake Mead National Recreation Area for perhaps two million years. For that long, this great river of the West fluctuated wildly with the seasons, in some years going on flooding rampages. The desire to control those floods and tap the river for irrigation and power generation led to the construction of Hoover Dam. Containment of 180 miles of the river, and creation of this playground in the desert, has happened in a little more than fifty years.

Above: Hoover Dam at night
Right: Near Boulder Beach, Nevada

LAKE MEAD NATIONAL RECREATION AREA
VISITOR INFORMATION

⟨ OPEN ⟩ Year-round

⟨ VISITOR CENTER ⟩ Alan Bible Visitor Center open 8:30 a.m.–4:30 p.m. daily except Thanksgiving, Christmas, and New Year's days; exhibits, audio-visual program, booksales

Information stations on Lake Mead: Overton Beach, Echo Bay, Las Vegas Bay, Temple Bar; on Lake Mohave at Cottonwood Cove and Katherine Landing

⟨ ENTRANCE FEE ⟩ Yes

⟨ CAMPING ⟩ Developed campgrounds for tents and RVs on Lake Mead at Boulder Beach, Callville Bay, Echo Bay, Las Vegas Bay, and Temple Bar; on Lake Mohave at Cottonwood

Cove and Katherine Landing. Backcountry camping allowed along lake shores, except along Lake Mead from Hoover Dam to Government Wash, in harbor areas, and where signed; backcountry camping elsewhere in recreation area only in designated areas— check with rangers

⟨ FISHING ⟩ Allowed with appropriate licenses

⟨ MARINAS ⟩ Lake Mead: Lake Mead Marina at Boulder Beach, Las Vegas Marina at Horsepower Cove, Callville Bay, Temple Bar, Echo Bay, Overton Beach

Lake Mohave: Cottonwood Cove, Katherine Landing, and Willow Beach

Marinas offer boat fuel and other services, rentals, food, and supplies; additional launch ramps accessible on each lake, depending on water levels

For Lake Mead sightseeing boat tours and charter boat service, contact concessioner at 702-293-6180

⟨ LODGING ⟩ On Lake Mead: Echo Bay, Lake Mead, and Temple Bar resorts; on Lake Mohave at Cottonwood Cove and Katherine Landing

⟨ NEARBY ACCOMMODATIONS I SERVICES ⟩ Las Vegas, Henderson, Boulder City, and Laughlin, Nevada, and Kingman and Bullhead City, Arizona

⟨ INFORMATION ⟩ Superintendent, Lake Mead National Recreation Area, 601 Nevada Way, Boulder City, NV 89005; phone: 702-293-8906; website: www.nps.gov/lame

The very name Mesa Verde conjures an image of serene, silent stone buildings reposing beneath sweeping sandstone alcoves.

Mesa Verde
NATIONAL PARK

In 1906, after much effort, Mesa Verde became a national park. It still holds the honor as the nation's first, and only, national park set aside for archeological treasures. The very name Mesa Verde conjures an image of serene, silent stone buildings reposing beneath sweeping sandstone alcoves. The famed cliff dwellings—Cliff Palace, Spruce Tree House, Balcony House, and Long House— are architectural masterpieces.

Yet these are only a handful of nearly 600 cliff dwellings, and these only a fraction of the more than 4,800 sites recorded in the park's 52,000 acres. This amazing collection earned Mesa Verde the prestigious United Nations designation as a World Heritage Cultural Site in 1978.

Mesa Verde deserves time, just to sit and gaze at the dwellings' intricate curves and lines, superb floor-to-ceiling towers, and details of T-shaped doorways. Time for a summer storm to release the intoxicating scent of moistened sagebrush. Time to think about how people lived in this place for more than 700 years and what might have caused them to depart.

Mesa Verde's earliest occupants, or at least those who left traces of their presence, came around A.D. 550. They were the Basketmakers, who wove willow basketry and dug pits into the hard ground, which they roofed and called home. Some of the early pithouses were located beneath the alcoves where the cliff dwellings now stand. Around A.D. 700 the ancestral Puebloans began to build mud and pole homes aboveground. Mortared masonry soon became the norm, and rooms were joined into pueblos.

The people cleared land on the mesatop for fields of corn, beans, and squash. Soils were deep enough, the growing season was long enough, and average precipitation—about 18 inches—was sufficient for a corn harvest. At places like Far View, they augmented the natural moisture with reservoirs. Domestic water came from springs. The piñon-juniper woodland furnished plentiful firewood and roof beams, while Gambel oak, serviceberry, and other trees and shrubs were additional sources of tools and food. Game animals such as mule deer and rabbits were hunted, while wild turkeys furnished feathers for warm robes during the cold winters.

As time went on, the ancestral Puebloans went back down into the alcoves. There they built the cliff dwellings for which Mesa Verde is famous. In fact, these beautiful stone homes—most built between the 1190s and 1270s—represent the last stages of their lives here. Some of the dwellings remained small, while others were expanded to more than 150 rooms. Underground, keyhole-shaped spaces called kivas were likely places for ceremonies and community gatherings. Tunnels connected some kivas to towers. This was a time of full flowering on Mesa Verde: most available land was farmed, stonework excelled in quality, and potters made exquisite black-on-white vessels.

Then, at the end of the 1200s, everything came to a halt. The Puebloans vacated the cliff dwellings, which had demanded so much work and craftsmanship. They left things behind, as if intending one day to return. But they never did. Instead, they moved south and ended up on the northern Rio Grande in New Mexico, at Zuni, and at Hopi in Arizona. Drought, depleted resources, social pressure, or a combination of these forces may have pushed, or pulled, them away after a successful 700-year tenure on the mesa.

Other American Indians followed. The Ute claimed nearly all of Colorado, and parts of their lands became Mesa Verde National Park. By the mid to late nineteenth century, a handful of miners, government surveyors, and ranchers—notably the Wetherill family from nearby Mancos—had "discovered" the spectacular cliff dwellings on the mesa. Wider public attention was kindled at the Columbian Exposition in Chicago in 1893. A group of women, who formed the Colorado Cliff Dwellings Association, successfully spearheaded efforts to preserve the antiquities in a park. Very soon after Mesa Verde's designation as a national park, the Smithsonian's Jesse Walter Fewkes excavated several sites.

In the summers of 2000 and 2002, forest fires blackened nearly half the park's acreage. Ironically, the fires revealed many new sites, most of them small scatters of pottery and stone but a few larger ones as well. And nearly a hundred years after Fewkes' excavations, archeologists performed detailed architectural documentation in Cliff Palace and Spruce Tree House. Their work revealed fewer total rooms than previously believed, and stimulated theories that each site housed two Puebloan societies simultaneously.

Entering these magnificent structures, where original building materials are still intact, visitors can ponder—and marvel—at how these resourceful farmers, hunters, and craftspeople lived on this high mesa for seven centuries.

Above: North courtyard, Spruce Tree House
Opposite: Cliff Palace
Opposite Right: Petroglyph, Pipe Shrine House

《 OPEN 》 Year-round; temporary road closures possible in winter

《 VISITOR CENTERS 》 Far View Visitor Center open 8 a.m.–5 p.m. mid-April to mid-October; tour tickets, exhibits, books, American Indian crafts, restrooms. Chapin Mesa Archeological Museum 8 a.m.–6:30 p.m. mid-April to mid-October, with shorter hours rest of year; exhibits, books, restrooms

《 ENTRANCE FEE 》 Yes; with additional fees for tickets for guided tours of most popular cliff dwellings

《 CAMPING 》 Morefield Campground, tents and RVs (hookups available); first-come, first-serve; open mid-April to mid-October; showers, laundry, general store, ranger station; call 800-449-2288 for information

《 SERVICES | FACILITIES 》 Food at Far View Lodge, Spruce Tree Terrace, and Morefield Campground. Lodging at Far View Lodge, mid April to early November, restaurant, cafeteria, gift shop; contact 800-449-2288 for reservations

《 NEARBY ACCOMMODATIONS | SERVICES 》 Cortez, Dolores, and Mancos, Colorado

《 INFORMATION 》 Superintendent, Mesa Verde National Park, P.O. Box 8, Mesa Verde National Park, CO 81330; phone: 970-529-4465; website: www.nps.gov/meve

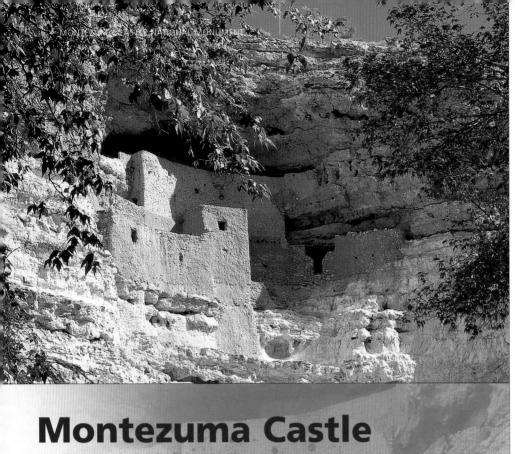

Montezuma Castle
NATIONAL MONUMENT

Tucked high in a cliffside alcove, Montezuma Castle overlooks Beaver Creek, a tributary of the Verde River in central Arizona.

The earthen walls of Montezuma Castle, nearly devoid of windows or doors, do indeed make the structure look like a "castle." But this was not the palace of an Aztec ruler, or of any royalty for that matter. It was simply home for a few families farming beside a creek 700 to 900 years ago.

Tucked high in a cliffside alcove, Montezuma Castle overlooks Beaver Creek, a tributary of the Verde River in central Arizona. The people who constructed the dwelling are known as the Sinagua, which in Spanish means "without water." Their brethren to the north, near present-day Flagstaff, did live in a land without water, which is where archeologists first identified the culture. But in the well-watered Verde Valley, they enjoyed the benefits bestowed by moisture, a mild climate, and a rich mix of resources.

Montezuma Castle itself may have housed only about thirty-five people, but a larger community of nearly 200 lived up and down Beaver Creek. They were farmers, who worked their floodplain fields and upland gardens with wooden digging sticks and stone hoes. Rain, snowmelt, and small irrigation ditches watered their crops—the classic southwestern triumvirate of corn, beans, and squash. Nature also provided a full array of resources—hackberry fruits and mesquite beans, yucca fibers, and the wood of streamside sycamores. Mule deer, squirrels, and even the occasional turtle or snake furnished protein.

Montezuma Castle's twenty rooms developed in stages within the massive protective alcove. Sometime around   1100, the first six rooms were placed in what would become the third floor. Rooms were erected above and below this central core; the parapet wall on the fifth floor was added, and finally three small rooms were located on top of one another, creating what looks like a multistory square tower. This was all accomplished by sheer manual labor, cutting the rock with stone axes, hauling water in clay pots up wooden ladders to the alcove ninety feet above the streambed, mixing it with clay, and mortaring the boulders in place.

Just around the corner is a larger structure known as "Castle A." It had forty-five rooms, and housed nearly a hundred people from   1200 to the early 1400s, a period when population began to concentrate in the middle Verde Valley. But a fire in the 1400s destroyed most of this dwelling; collapsed walls and foundations are all that remain. Despite what was likely a bountiful life here, the Sinagua left the Verde Valley in the early 1400s, settling in villages at what are now Hopi and Zuni.

Montezuma Castle received little attention until the late 1880s. Then Edgar Mearns, Army surgeon and accomplished naturalist, came from nearby Fort Verde and dug in some rooms. His efforts did not reveal much—broken pottery and stone implements. A few years later a local group repaired the disintegrating walls, and in 1906 Montezuma Castle was designated one of the nation's first national monuments. Full protection for the site came in 1947, and by 1951 visitors could no longer enter the dwellings because of their fragile nature.

Above: Montezuma Castle, one of the best-preserved cliff dwellings in North America

> The basic difference is that natural bridges require a flowing stream to make them, while arches do not.

Natural Bridges
NATIONAL MONUMENT

In 1992, two tons of sandstone blocks thundered to the ground off Kachina Bridge in Natural Bridges National Monument. This event provided dramatic proof that the erosion that created this natural bridge and the two others within the monument is an ongoing process.

Prospector Cass Hite "discovered" these geologic wonders as he and three men, including a Paiute named Indian Joe, explored White and Armstrong canyons in southeast Utah in 1883. Old Cass, without much imagination, bestowed the names of President, Senator, and Congressman to the three stone bridges and made their existence known to the nation. *National Geographic* magazine furnished more publicity, including illustrations, and in 1908 President Theodore Roosevelt established Natural Bridges as Utah's first national monument. Government surveyor William Douglass soon arrived and determined that the names of the bridges could better reflect the people who once lived in the region—ancestors of today's Hopi and other Pueblo Indians. Douglass chose Hopi names—Sipapu, Kachina, and Owachomo—which remain today.

The three spans occur about three miles apart down the canyons, each framing classic views of blue sky. Sipapu is the largest, with a height of 220 feet and a span of 268 feet. (It is the second largest natural bridge in the world, exceeded only by Rainbow Bridge in nearby Glen Canyon.) Kachina stands in the middle, 210 feet high and 204 feet edge to edge. Smallest is Owachomo, 106 feet high with a 180-foot span.

Some people might question superlatives, pointing to Kolob Arch in Zion National Park and Landscape Arch in namesake Arches. But they are arches, not natural bridges. The basic difference is that natural bridges require a flowing stream to make them, while arches do not.

Sipapu, Kachina, and Owachomo were etched out of the Cedar Mesa sandstone of White and Armstrong canyons. Streams cut down into the uplifted mesa, meandering and becoming set in their course as they cut deeper. As the meanders became more pronounced, thin fins of sandstone were left between each bend. Torrential seasonal flash floods tore down these canyons (and still do), carrying tons of rock debris that gnawed into the fins. Finally the weak spots gave way, a bridge started to form, and then was widened and enlarged by the continuing force of water flowing beneath it. In contrast, an arch is formed by water eroding within the rock, with the help of wind.

However formed, the bridges show nature's artistry at her best.

Above: Sipapu Bridge spans 268 feet

NATURAL BRIDGES NATIONAL MONUMENT
VISITOR INFORMATION

‹ OPEN › Year-round

‹ VISITOR CENTER › Open 8 a.m.–5 p.m. daily with extended summer hours; closed Thanksgiving, Christmas, and New Year's days; exhibits, booksales, slide program

‹ ENTRANCE FEE › Yes

‹ CAMPING › Small campground for tents and RVs under 28 feet; first-come, first-serve, no drinking water

‹ SCENIC DRIVES › 9-mile Bridge View Drive

‹ SERVICES | FACILITIES › Restrooms, water (only at visitor center), picnic area

‹ NEARBY ACCOMMODATIONS | SERVICES › Blanding and Mexican Hat, Utah

‹ INFORMATION › Superintendent, Natural Bridges National Monument, HC 60, Box 1, Lake Powell, UT 84533; phone: 435-692-1234; website: www.nps.gov/nabr

NAVAJO NATIONAL MONUMENT
VISITOR INFORMATION

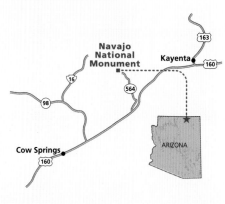

《 OPEN 》 Year-round

《 VISITOR CENTER 》 Open 8 a.m.–5 p.m. every day, with extended summer hours; closed Thanksgiving, Christmas, and New Year's days; exhibits, video, booksales, American Indian arts and crafts sold next door

《 ENTRANCE FEE 》 No

《 CAMPING 》 Small campground for tents and RVs 28 feet and less (no hookups), first-come, first-serve, open year-round

《 SERVICES | FACILITIES 》 Restrooms, water, picnic area

《 NEARBY ACCOMMODATIONS | SERVICES 》 Black Mesa and Kayenta, Arizona

《 INFORMATION 》 Superintendent, Navajo National Monument, HC 71, P.O. Box 3, Tonalea, AZ 86044; phone: 928-672-2700; website: www.nps.gov/nava

The names Keet Seel and Betatakin resonate among the list of the Southwest's crown-jewel archeological sites.

Navajo
NATIONAL MONUMENT

Betatakin cliff dwelling, occupied by ancestral Puebloans in the 1200s

Kayenta black-on-white olla

The names Keet Seel and Betatakin resonate among the list of the Southwest's crown-jewel archeological sites. These two deserve their renown, for they are like gems set in the vastness of the sandstone canyons of the Four Corners country.

Keet Seel was the primary motivation for the federal government to set aside Navajo National Monument in 1909, a small park surrounded by the Navajo Nation. Betatakin was found five months after that. For visitors who walk to Betatakin with a park ranger, or who have the time to make the more demanding overnight hike to Keet Seel, the sight of either one is unforgettable.

The park sits high on the Shonto Plateau at 7,000 feet above sea level, amid the seemingly endless Tsegi Canyon system on the greater Colorado Plateau. Winters can be snowy and frigid, summers pleasantly warm, the clear air fragrant with piñon pine and juniper. Box

elder and aspen fill the shaded, moister side canyons, while sagebrush and buffaloberry lend soft gray tones to drier ground.

A welter of cliffs, benches, and arroyos tendrils into the plateau. Betatakin sits in a high arched alcove up in a small side canyon of Tsegi. Sometime between ᴀᴅ 1250 and 1267, people were lured here and built a series of small masonry houses in the cliffside—thus the Navajo name Betatakin, which translates to "alcove dwelling." The alcove had been used earlier, but this relatively sudden burst of domestic activity was a sign that something had attracted the ancestral Puebloans of the Kayenta area here. Increasing population and the need for more farmland may have dictated their moves farther upcanyon.

Keet Seel was inhabited for a longer time. Evidence of occupation dates as early as ᴀᴅ 950. A second village, started around ᴀᴅ 1250, is the largest in the Tsegi Canyon system.

Keet Seel's 155 rooms perch beneath the soaring sandstone ceiling, facing a "street" or walkway along the entire length of the alcove. Masonry rooms, granaries, and sacred spaces called kivas are part of the complex. These people also devoted considerable time to making beautiful black-on-white pottery of coiled and smoothed clay.

The residents of Betatakin and Keet Seel left for good after ᴀᴅ 1300. Drought, deeper arroyo-cutting, overpopulation, or social stress may have combined to force them out. When modern-day Hopi visit these villages, which they call Kawestima and Talastima, they see the homes of their ancestors, the *hisatsinom*.

Through the years the monument's remoteness has helped protect the sites. That intimate, quieter ambiance keeps Navajo National Monument a shining jewel.

Today, people most value Organ Pipe's essence of desert—the dry air, stark mountains, and plants and animals so admirably adapted to their environment.

Organ Pipe Cactus
NATIONAL MONUMENT

Among the practical tips given to visitors to Organ Pipe Cactus National Monument is how to extract spiny cactus stems from one's flesh. "Use two sticks, a pair of pliers, tweezers, or a comb to flip the joint away from you," the guidebooks advise.

Though visitors are discouraged from putting themselves within spines' reach, unpleasant encounters can happen. In a park that boasts twenty-six species of cacti, knowing how to remove those wicked spines is useful.

The large organ pipe cactus gives this 330,000-acre park in far southern Arizona its name. A warm-desert species of Mexico, organ pipe cacti just cross over into the United States in this park. Long fluted green stems rise from the base of the plant, and it produces a delicious edible fruit.

First-time visitors strive to separate organ pipe cactus from the more famous and plentiful saguaro cactus, which also grows in the park. The range of the saguaro fairly well describes the bounds of the Sonoran Desert, one of four major deserts in

North America. Organ Pipe Cactus National Monument is a showcase of the Sonoran Desert, not only for the outstanding columnar cacti but also for a fascinating cast of other plant and animal characters.

Here the lower Sonoran Desert meets upland, creating a fertile zone of mixing. Plant communities are sorted by rainfall, temperature, topography, and soils. The lowest—and hottest—valleys stretching between the mountains support olive creosote bush and dusky-green bursage. The velvet-leaved brittlebush, saltbush, and foothills palo verde fill in other low areas. Moving up onto the bajadas and hillsides, the upland communities contain saguaro and organ pipe cactus, the infamous cholla, prickly pear, and green-barked palo verde trees. At the highest and best-watered elevations grow jojoba, agave, and even the occasional juniper. Added to this healthy diversity are a few representatives from Mexico's Gulf Coast—the shaggy-bearded senita, or old man cactus; elephant trees; and limber bush.

People flock to this desert in March and April to see dazzling wildflower displays. After wet winters, the rugged ochre hills and slopes are splashed with gold poppies, pink owl's clover, blue lupines, and sunny yellow globes of brittlebush. The cacti bloom mostly in summer, when people tend to avoid this intemperate place.

The valleys and mountains of Organ Pipe are filled with birds. In the cool hours of early morning and toward evening, white-winged doves, Gila woodpeckers, and cactus wrens are about. Road-runners dart from shrub to shrub, and red-tailed hawks perch on the tips of saguaro arms. Rarer are sightings of reptiles—a beaded Gila monster along

a dry wash or a diamondback rattlesnake coiled beside a boulder. Coyotes and javelinas are always on the hunt for food, while bighorn sheep frequent the rocky slopes. Kangaroo rats scurry along runways at night, and industrious packrats gather cholla joints to armor their nests.

Quitobaquito, a spring-fed pond in the southwest corner of the park, is an oasis amid the sere desert. Cottonwoods shade the still pool, and bulrushes rim the banks. Bats, pupfish, herons, mud turtles, and mountain lions are lured to this life-giving water. People were drawn here too—the Tohono O'odham and Hia-Ced O'odham lived, camped, and farmed beside what they called 'A'al Waipia, Little Wells. The O'odham desert knowledge would have well served Euro-Americans who suffered along the torrid stretches of El Camino del Diablo, the Devil's Highway. Spanish priests, miners, and a few Anglo ranchers left some vestiges of their presence here.

Today, people most value Organ Pipe's essence of desert—the dry air, stark mountains, and plants and animals so admirably adapted to their environment.

Above: Organ pipe cactus with the Ajo Mountains in the background
Left: Regal horned lizard

Organ Pipe Cactus National Monument celebrates the life and landscape of the Sonoran Desert.

Above: Barrel cactus blooms

ORGAN PIPE CACTUS NATIONAL MONUMENT
VISITOR INFORMATION

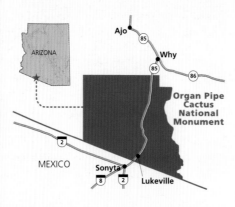

《 OPEN 》 Year-round, October to April best time to visit

《 VISITOR CENTER 》 Open 8 a.m.–5 p.m.

daily except Christmas and summer holidays; exhibits, slide show, booksales

《 ENTRANCE FEE 》 Yes

《 CAMPING 》 Twin Peaks Campground open all year, first-come, first-serve, no RVs longer than 35 feet; Alamo Campground, 4 sites, for tents, pickup trucks with campers, or vans only; commercial campgrounds in towns of Lukeville and Why, Arizona

《 SERVICES | FACILITIES 》 Restrooms, water, picnic areas

《 NEARBY ACCOMMODATIONS | SERVICES 》 Ajo, Lukeville, and Why, Arizona, and Sonoyta, Mexico

《 INFORMATION 》 Superintendent, Organ Pipe Cactus National Monument, 10 Organ Pipe Drive, Ajo, AZ 85321; phone: 520-387-6849; website: www.nps.gov/orpi

By the 1400s, Pecos had attained a dominant position in the region. From its location on the high ridge, and with an enclosing rock wall, the site appeared fortresslike.

Pecos
NATIONAL HISTORICAL PARK

For thousands of years people of different cultures lived at what is now Pecos National Historical Park between New Mexico's Sangre de Cristo Mountains and the Great Plains.

To this strategic passageway on the eastern rim of the Pueblo world, Plains tribes brought slaves, flint, shell, hides, and skins in exchange for turquoise, corn, and pottery of the pueblos. The people of Pecos acted as wholesalers and distributors in this age-old economic system. Less tangible but no less important was the exchange of news and ideas among these far-flung groups when they converged at Pecos.

The earliest residents of Pecos dug pit homes along drainages about A.D. 800. Three centuries later, ancestral Puebloans were building small masonry villages aboveground. But in the 1300s, the people concentrated in what grew to be a five-story, sprawling 600-room dwelling of 2,000 residents—known today as Pecos Pueblo.

By the 1400s, Pecos had attained a dominant position in the region. From its location on the high ridge, and with an enclosing rock wall, the site appeared fortresslike. The wall may have controlled access, letting traders into the pueblo by day but not at night.

More than twenty kivas—places of ritual and ceremony—were part of Pecos. Visitors can climb down a wooden ladder into a restored kiva, emerging in the dark, cool confines of the round room with its smooth-plastered walls.

When the first Spaniards entered New Mexico they too stopped at Pecos, then known as Cicuye. Francisco Vázquez de Coronado's expedition arrived in 1541 and was met with friendship. In 1584, another conquistador described the pueblo "enclosed and protected by a wall and large houses, and by tiers of walkways which look out on the countryside. On these they keep their offensive and defensive arms: bows, arrows, shields, spears, and war clubs."

In 1598 the subjugating Spaniards came to stay. The first Franciscan mission church was completed in 1625, but it was burned and the priest killed during the Pueblo Revolt in August of 1680. A second church and attached convento were built in 1717 upon the foundations of the first church; some original adobe can still be seen in its transept. Finally, in 1838, the few remaining residents went to their cousin pueblo of Jemez, ending five centuries of occupation of this important town.

In 1915 the ruins of Pecos became the location of a pioneering archeological excavation. Fresh from Harvard with a shiny new doctorate, Alfred Vincent Kidder spent twelve seasons in the pueblo, revealing a complex overlay of long occupation at the site. The first "Pecos Conference" was held at his field camp in 1927, where Kidder and colleagues devised the first chronology and nomenclature of early southwestern life, a major leap in the science of archeology that is still in use today.

The newest portion of the park, the Forked Lightning Ranch, came through a gift to the National Park Service from actress Greer Garson and her husband E. E. Fogelson in 1993.

Above: A kiva in front of the second church at Pecos

PECOS NATIONAL HISTORICAL PARK
VISITOR INFORMATION

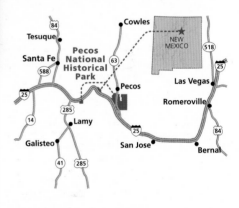

《 OPEN 》 Year-round except Christmas and New Year's days

《 VISITOR CENTER 》 8 a.m.–6 p.m. Memorial Day to Labor Day; 8 a.m.–5 p.m. rest of year, exhibits, booksales, film; trail through site open same hours

《 ENTRANCE FEE 》 Yes

《 TOURS 》 Ranger-guided tours offered daily in summer and by special arrangement the rest of the year; phone 505-757-6414 ext. 1 for schedule and reservations

《 CAMPING 》 None in park; nearest in Santa Fe National Forest

《 SERVICES I FACILITIES 》 Restrooms, water, picnic area

《 NEARBY ACCOMMODATIONS I SERVICES 》 Pecos, Santa Fe, and Las Vegas, New Mexico

《 INFORMATION 》 Superintendent, Pecos National Historical Park, P.O. Box 418, Pecos, NM 87552; phone: 505-757-6414; website: www.nps.gov/peco

The most noticeable evidence of this strikingly different past glitters all over the ground. It is petrifed wood, trees turned to stone.

PETRIFIED FOREST NATIONAL PARK
VISITOR INFORMATION

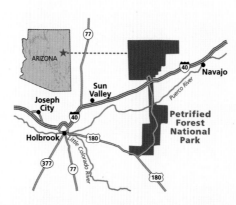

‹ OPEN › Year-round, 8 a.m.–5 p.m., extended hours in summer; closed Christmas Day

‹ VISITOR CENTERS › Painted Desert Visitor Center at park's north entrance: 8 a.m.–5 p.m., call for extended hours; exhibits, audio-visual program, books; Painted Desert Inn Museum open 9 a.m.–5 p.m.; exhibits, booksales in historic building; Rainbow Forest Museum at park's south entrance open 8 a.m.–5 p.m., call for extended hours; exhibits, snack bar, gift shop

‹ ENTRANCE FEE › Yes

‹ CAMPING › None in park

‹ SERVICES | FACILITIES › Restrooms, water, picnic area, cafeteria, gift shop, gasoline

‹ NEARBY ACCOMMODATIONS | SERVICES › Holbrook, Arizona, and Gallup, New Mexico

‹ INFORMATION › Superintendent, Petrified Forest National Park, P.O. Box 2217, Petrified Forest, AZ 86028; phone: 928-524-6228; website: www.nps.gov/pefo

Petrified Forest
NATIONAL PARK

Visitors to Petrified Forest today must possess a healthy dose of imagination to envision the environment that predated this high, dry, silent land. The mental journey must go back 225 million years or so to the Triassic Period, when what is now northern Arizona was near the equator. Tall tropical trees held sway in the highlands, with an undergrowth of broad ferns, lush cycads, and huge horsetails. An astonishing assortment of animals inhabited the land and water of this green world, including some of the earliest plant- and meat-eating dinosaurs, giant amphibians, flying lizards, fish, clams, snails, and experiments in the up-and-coming group known as mammals.

The most noticeable evidence of this strikingly different past glitters all over the ground. It is petrified wood, trees turned to stone, the reason this park was set aside. The Triassic-aged trees toppled and were carried down flooding streams, collecting over the years in what must have been monstrous logjams. Sediments and volcanic ash, blown and washed in, buried the fresh trees and prevented their rapid decay. The accumulation of the mud, silt, sand, and ash created what is known as the Chinle Formation, the soft striped hills that make up Petrified Forest National Park and the wilderness of the Painted Desert in its northern section.

Over time, silica-laden waters replaced the cellulose in the wood of the trees, crystallizing into quartz, jasper, and chalcedony. Thus, the wood was "petrified" into gemlike hues of reds, oranges, purples, and blacks, now gorgeously revealed in cross sections of the trees.

Along the Long Logs trail at the south end of the park, tree trunks 100 feet or more in length have been preserved. In other places, the trees broke cleanly into rounds that look as if they were cut by a saw. The petrified wood clogs drainages where the soft badland clays have eroded out around them, or it perches on pedestals of clay as if placed by a careful hand.

These fossils, and many less obvious ones, have lured professional and amateur paleontologists to Petrified Forest for years and have allowed scientists to fill in more details of the past environments and evolution. An exciting find occurred in the park in 1984—bones of one of the earliest dinosaurs known, a creature fondly named "Gertie." The remains of a whole menagerie of crawling, swimming, and flying animals have been unearthed in Petrified Forest, along with delicate fossils of early plants. Paleontologists still comb the melting hills for more clues to this Triassic world.

Humans have passed through and lived in this sunstruck land for a very long time, perhaps as long as 10,000 years ago. Paleo-Indians and then Archaic people lived off the land; hunting big game and then turning to smaller prey such as cottontail rabbits and prairie dogs. The greens and seeds of tansy mustard and ricegrass also added to their diets. Later folk settled down to grow corn, first living in pithouses then building aboveground structures of sandstone slabs and blocks of petrified wood, such as Puerco Pueblo and Agate House, excavated sites open to visitors. Generations of people left catalogs of their lives on burnished boulders; some of these petroglyphs are symbols that appear to have been deliberately positioned as markers of summer

solstice and other significant celestial events.

The first Euro-Americans, an expedition of Spaniards in 1540, passed near Petrified Forest but did not stay. Federal government surveyors charting a course for a possible cross-country railroad line came through in December 1853. The amount of petrified wood they saw led them to give the name Lithodendron, meaning "stone trees," to the major wash that drains the northern part of the park. The Atlantic & Pacific Railroad did choose this route, along the 35th Parallel, completing tracks through northern Arizona in 1882. For the next forty years, that's how visitors came to see Petrified Forest. Route 66, the famed Mother Road, paralleled the same route and opened the region to auto travelers. A favorite stop was the Painted Desert Inn, built in 1924 at Kachina Point, where visitors savored fantastic views of the many-hued hills outside, while indoors they could admire the painted murals of Hopi artist Fred Kabotie. Most recently, Interstate 40 has plunged through the corridor and now ushers in the majority of visitors.

With tons of petrified wood rapidly disappearing at the hands of collectors, the federal government set aside Petrified Forest as a park in 1906 to protect this valuable national wealth. Too many people still cannot resist the lure of a small piece here and a chip there for a souvenir. Each year the pilfering of petrified wood adds up—visitors should be aware of the park's "zero tolerance" policy for such illegal collection.

Fortunately, this world-class treasure of petrified wood still resides in this national park, a beautiful and valuable testament to another time in the earth's history.

Opposite: Petrified logs jam a drainage at Blue Mesa.
Top: Remains of a Triassic forest overlook the Painted Desert.
Above: Four-wing saltbush seedling in the Painted Desert

The lava from those volcanoes cooled and created a rock surface upon which Native people left their mark in the forms of birds, snakes, circles, spirals, stars, masks, and handprints. . . .

More than a hundred thousand years ago, volcanoes erupted in what is now central New Mexico. The lava from those volcanoes cooled and created a rock surface upon which Native people left their mark in the forms of birds, snakes, circles, spirals, stars, masks, and handprints pecked in stark white onto black boulders. Some 20,000 images have been identified and are protected within Petroglyph National Monument.

The lava welled up along the Rio Grande Rift, the spreading zone that formed the valley through which the great river flows. Five volcanic cinder cones—Butte, Bond, Vulcan, Black, and JA—and seventeen-mile-long West Mesa now rise above the grass and shrub lands on the west side of present-day Albuquerque. Chipping away at the patinated veneer, using a single rock as a hammer

headdresses. The nearby Macaw Trail features an etching of a macaw. The feathers of these tropical parrots were an important trade item among southwestern Pueblo people, desired for their brilliant colors and ceremonial uses. Another large, dominant petroglyph is interpreted as the seed pod of a yucca, a plant that furnished everything from soap to fiber.

The meaning and significance of the petroglyphs is often best left to the eye of the beholder. For modern-day Pueblo people who come here, these images of natural beings and clan symbols are inspired with stories and held in highest esteem. As one elder has said, "each of these rocks is alive" in this place of "spirits, guardians . . . [and] medicine."

Petroglyph
NATIONAL MONUMENT

or with another as a chisel, people left an astounding outdoor record over thousands of years.

The earliest known petroglyphs are abstract designs by hunter-gatherers who paused here 2,000 to 3,000 years ago. Some of them settled down, growing small patches of corn in the warmer washes at the foot of the mesas. Over the next millennium, people built permanent structures, grew more food, and added many more images.

Most of the petroglyphs in the park fit into what archeologists describe as the Rio Grande Style, which developed suddenly around A.D. 1300 and continued into the 1600s. By that time people were living in nearly forty pueblo villages along the middle Rio Grande. After 1692, Spanish settlers placed their own marks, often in the form of Christian crosses and sheep brands. Less considerate newcomers have left bullet holes and other defacements.

In Boca Negra Canyon two miles north of the park visitor center, three trails exhibit a wide range of petroglyphs. Intriguing four-pointed stars, shields, figures of cats and dragonflies, spirals, circles, and horned masks can be seen along the Mesa Point Trail. On the mesatop, at 5,280 feet elevation, a sea of tiled roofs fills the view out to the east and south, dwellings of the most recent culture to inhabit the valley. It is instructive to contrast the sights and sounds of the modern Sunbelt city of Albuquerque while standing amid the vestiges of past lives. A low rock structure on top of the mesa may be an old ceremonial spot or a historic corral.

Along the Cliff Base Trail, hikers see faces decorated with head ornaments and feathered

PETROGLYPH NATIONAL MONUMENT
VISITOR INFORMATION

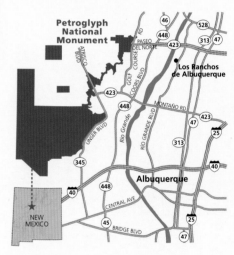

⟨ OPEN ⟩ Year-round except Thanksgiving, Christmas, and New Year's days

⟨ VISITOR CENTER ⟩ Las Imágenes Visitor Center open 8 a.m.–5 p.m.; information and book sales; check schedule of ranger-led walks

⟨ ENTRANCE FEE ⟩ None; parking fee at Boca Negra Canyon entrance

⟨ CAMPING ⟩ None in park; nearest in Albuquerque, Coronado State Monument, and Cibola National Forest

⟨ SERVICES I FACILITIES ⟩ Restrooms; water at picnic area at Boca Negra, no water at Rinconada or Volcanoes day-use areas

⟨ NEARBY ACCOMMODATIONS I SERVICES ⟩ Albuquerque, New Mexico

⟨ INFORMATION ⟩ Superintendent, Petroglyph National Monument, 6001 Unser Blvd. NW, Albuquerque, NM 87120; phone: 505-899-0205; website: www.nps.gov/petr

Left: Petroglyphs carved into basalt boulders, Piedras Marcadas Canyon

Today, the dining room table is set at Winsor Castle, quilts are on the beds, and the cool water of Pipe Spring still trickles, soft and inviting, at this high-desert oasis.

Pipe Spring
NATIONAL MONUMENT

For hundreds of years, Pueblo and Southern Paiute people lived and farmed at a place called Matungwa'vu—a bountiful upwelling of water flowing from the red rock of the Vermilion Cliffs on the Arizona Strip.

Today the place is known as Pipe Spring, so named by Mormons who colonized this remote country in the nineteenth century. James Whitmore started ranching at Pipe Spring in 1863. While living in a crude dugout, he managed to plant grapevines and fruit trees and build a corral. Conflict among the Mormons, Ute, and Navajo threatened the region's remote settlements throughout the 1860s. Navajo raiders killed Whitmore near his dugout in 1866, and in response Mormon militia executed seven Southern Paiute. Later, Pipe Spring served as a base for the militia in encounters with the Navajo.

In 1870 Bishop Anson Perry Winsor followed the orders of church leader Brigham Young and began superintending construction of a substantial fortified structure at Pipe Spring, for defense against possible Navajo raids and for a ranch. Mormon families were expected to tithe a tenth of their income to the church. Those tithes could take the form of livestock, and Young believed the grasslands around Pipe Spring would support a tithing cattle herd.

So Winsor Castle was built, of rock quarried from local sandstone and pine timbers freighted in from Mount Trumbull many miles to the south. Masons, carpenters, and blacksmiths spent two years building it.

The tall structure had two wooden gates on either end, wide enough to permit a wagon to enter. The stout walls enclosed two houses separated by a spacious courtyard, with parlor, kitchen, meeting and guest room, and bedrooms. To protect the precious water source, a room was built over the spring; the 56-degree water kept the milk, cream, butter, and cheese cool. The dairy products produced at Pipe Spring were carried every two weeks to the builders of the Mormon temple at St. George, Utah.

Winsor Castle was a welcome waystop for travelers crossing the Arizona Strip, the empty, windswept quarter of northwest Arizona Territory between the Grand Canyon and the Utah border. Famed geologist John Wesley Powell watched the groundbreaking for the fort, and his surveying team bunked in the small West Cabin beside Winsor Castle in 1872. Among frequent visitors was Jacob Hamblin, the Mormon missionary and pathfinder who had known of Pipe Spring as early as the 1850s, and who is often credited with naming the place. Hamblin no doubt learned of the spring from Paiute guides, who had long claimed the valued waters.

Despite the benefit of the fort and ranch to Mormon settlers and travelers, their arrival was detrimental to the Kaibab Band of Paiute. The Kaibab were excluded from the water source that had been keenly important to their existence. Other changes brought by settlers devastated the Kaibab population, shrinking from 1,200 in 1860 to barely 100 individuals in 1900.

Stephen Mather, first director of the National Park Service, was convinced of the site's historical significance. In 1923 President Warren Harding declared forty acres as Pipe Spring National Monument.

Today, the dining room table is set at Winsor Castle, quilts are on the beds, and the cool water of Pipe Spring still trickles, soft and inviting, at this high-desert oasis.

Above: Blacksmith Shop and Harness room, constructed in 1868

PIPE SPRING NATIONAL MONUMENT
VISITOR INFORMATION

❰ OPEN ❱ Year-round, closed Thanksgiving, Christmas, and New Year's days

❰ VISITOR CENTER ❱ Open 8 a.m–5 p.m. with extended summer hours; exhibits, video, book-sales. Shared with Kaibab Band of Paiute

❰ ENTRANCE FEE ❱ Yes

❰ TRAILS ❱ One-half mile self-guiding loop trail around grounds; ranger-led tours of Winsor Castle offered every half hour 8 a.m.–4 :30 p.m. summer; 8:30 a.m.–4 p.m. winter

❰ CAMPING ❱ None on site; campground ½ mile away on Kaibab Paiute Indian Reservation, also in Kaibab National Forest and North Rim of Grand Canyon

❰ SERVICES I FACILITIES ❱ Water, restrooms

❰ NEARBY ACCOMMODATIONS I SERVICES ❱ Fredonia, Arizona, and Kanab, Utah

❰ INFORMATION ❱ Superintendent, Pipe Spring National Monument, HC 65, Box 5, 406 N. Pipe Spring Rd., Fredonia, AZ 86022; phone: 928-643-7105; website: www.nps.gov/pisp

This great arc of sandstone sits astride Bridge Canyon on Utah's southern border. It is the world's largest natural bridge—spanning 275 feet and 290 feet high.

Rainbow Bridge
NATIONAL MONUMENT

Rainbow Bridge unquestionably ranks as an extraordinary natural wonder. It is also a portal and an altar. This great arc of sandstone sits astride Bridge Canyon on Utah's southern border. It is the world's largest natural bridge—spanning 275 feet and 290 feet high. As a portal, Rainbow Bridge marks a momentous entrance into a twisted maze of canyon country. Its nearly symmetrical opening frames Navajo Mountain, a forested dome that rises to 10,388 feet. And it is a place that neighboring tribes—the Navajo, Hopi, San Juan Southern Paiute, Kaibab Paiute, and White Mesa Ute—consider sacred.

First a little geologic pedigree. Rainbow Bridge sits on a foundation of Kayenta Sandstone, but the bulk of the span is Navajo Sandstone. The Navajo, premier rock of the Southwest's canyon country, was formed from billowing sand dunes a thousand feet thick that covered the land 170 to 190 million years ago. Geologist Herbert Gregory, who traveled on foot and by pack animal through this rugged land in the early 1900s, proclaimed that the "intricacy and grandeur of the stream-carved sculpture are unexcelled in any other part of the Plateau province." It was Gregory who described and named the Navajo Sandstone as a formal geologic formation.

It takes a stream to make a natural bridge. In this case, Bridge Creek flowed off Navajo Mountain bound for the Colorado River. The stream became entrenched as the land rose around it, cutting a sinuous canyon into the Navajo Sandstone. When the creek met the underlying Kayenta formation, its work became harder. Wandering for a time, it broke through a neck of a meander loop. The water then charged downstream, gnawing at the sandstone and undermining the base, until the bridge was formed.

This process took millions of years, and Rainbow Bridge stood hidden in the plateau wilderness several more million years before people ever saw it. Early inhabitants of the Colorado Plateau certainly had a view. Later, the Navajo and Paiute moved into this part of the world. In 1909, Navajos first told traders Louisa and John Wetherill of Nonnezoshe, the "rainbow turned to stone." John Wetherill had been showing a few people around the area, and he informed archeologist Byron Cummings of the existence of the bridge. In August 1909, Wetherill, Cummings, his young nephew Neil Judd, surveyor William Douglass, and Paiute guides Nasja Begay and Jim Mike set out to find it.

They took five days to make the rigorous, hot trip over trackless land, arriving on August 14. From that point, the story rouses debate: Who among the group first spied Rainbow Bridge? Judd credited his uncle, Byron Cummings. Writer Zane Grey said it was John Wetherill. Others have maintained that William Douglass was first. None, however, would have found it without the Paiute guides. A year later, President William Howard Taft declared the 160-acre Rainbow Bridge National Monument.

Today, a trip to Rainbow Bridge is far less arduous. The waters of Lake Powell reach up into the canyon where the bridge stands, and most visitors now come by boat, then walk a short trail to gaze upon the spectacle.

RAINBOW BRIDGE NATIONAL MONUMENT
VISITOR INFORMATION

❰ OPEN ❱ Year-round. Rainbow Bridge accessible only by 50-mile boat trip on Lake Powell or 13-mile hike around Navajo Mountain. Boat tours available through park concessioner, phone 800-528-6154

❰ VISITOR CENTER ❱ None; park rangers on duty at Rainbow Bridge daily from Memorial Day through Labor Day. Additional information can be obtained at Carl Hayden Visitor Center at Glen Canyon Dam and others in Glen Canyon National Recreation Area

❰ ENTRANCE FEE ❱ No, but must pay entrance fee for Glen Canyon National Recreation Area

❰ CAMPING ❱ Not allowed in monument; nearest on shores of Lake Powell or elsewhere in Glen Canyon National Recreation Area

❰ SERVICES I FACILITIES ❱ Courtesy boat dock and vault toilets at Rainbow Bridge; nearest ranger station at Dangling Rope Marina on Lake Powell, staffed intermittently. Marina open year-round, with restrooms, water, boat fuel, first aid, and limited supplies

❰ NEARBY ACCOMMODATIONS I SERVICES ❱ Page, Arizona, or Bullfrog, Utah

❰ INFORMATION ❱ Superintendent, Rainbow Bridge National Monument, Box 1507, Page, AZ 86040; phone: 928-608-6404; website: www.nps.gov/rabr

Above: Rainbow Bridge took millions of years to form.

> One vegetative marvel—
> the saguaro cactus—is the
> signature of the park and
> the reason it was created.

Saguaro
NATIONAL PARK

Some say that to live in the desert you must get over the color green. Not so in the Sonoran Desert. One of the best places to appreciate that verdure is Saguaro National Park in southern Arizona.

One vegetative marvel—the saguaro cactus— is the signature of the park and the reason it was created. With eleven inches of rainfall spread almost equally between winter and summer, this part of the Sonoran Desert holds the world's finest collection of saguaros.

Two sections—Saguaro West and Saguaro East—make up this 91,000-acre park, separated by the city of Tucson. The west side is a little lower and warmer than the east, providing nearly ideal conditions for saguaros and other warmth-loving species like ironwood trees. The east district features good stands of saguaros too, best seen along the Cactus Forest Drive; it also holds the higher Rincon Mountains that support oak, juniper, and pine.

Saguaros are amazing plants. They stand like sentinels on the hillsides, arms beseeching the sky,

some mighty elders reaching forty feet tall and weighing ten tons. More amazing is the fact that one of these giants grows from a seed no larger than a drop of ink. A given population of saguaros produces billions of seeds each year, but only a handful will sprout and grow. Those seeds that remain after animals have had their feasts stay in the ground until the right conditions of moisture and temperature arrive. Once germinated, a saguaro seedling is vulnerable; to survive, it needs the shelter of a boulder or a "nurse" tree during those young tender years. Growth is painfully slow: a foot in fifteen years, seven feet in fifty years. Those with arms are at least seventy-five years old, and the oldest may live 150 years before succumbing to lightning, wind, drought, or freezes.

Saguaros store water in their succulent tissue, and accordion-like pleats along the stems let them shrink and swell as moisture decreases and increases. A woody ribbed skeleton supports the tissue, and a wide-spreading, shallow root system

anchors the plants in rocky ground.

Nubby flower buds appear on the tips of saguaro arms in May and June, opening into luscious creamy-white blossoms that crown the branches. Each flower blooms and wilts within twenty-four hours, so bats and bees waste no time spreading the wealth of pollen from one flower to another. Bulbous red fruits jammed with black seeds appear by late June and July, just as the summer monsoon rains traditionally start to pelt the desert.

Saguaro fruits were a life-sustaining food for the O'odham people of the Sonoran Desert. They cooked the fruit into jam and drank the fermented juice during an annual rain-bringing ceremony. The Hohokam, who lived here from around A.D. 600 to 1450, used saguaro juice as an acid to etch shell. Rocks at Signal Hill in Saguaro West bear Hohokam petroglyphs, perhaps their way of beseeching the gods for rain. While people depended on saguaros, so do desert animals. Gila woodpeckers and elf owls nest in cavities in the cactus, and doves and packrats devour the fruit and seeds.

Coyotes, lizards, cottontails, bobcats, rattlesnakes, and tarantulas are common denizens of this desert. Even amphibians, notably spadefoot toads, live here, waiting for the rains so they can complete their compressed life cycles.

The park's mountain ranges contain deposits of copper and silver sought by miners in the nineteenth century. Their roads and diggings are still visible in places on both the west and east sides. Ranchers introduced livestock, and over-grazing took a toll on the fragile desert environment. Humans have had other impacts here, most recently the rapid urbanization pressing against the park's boundaries. In 1994, Saguaro National Monument became Saguaro National Park, continuing to assure a sanctuary for the stately saguaro cactus and all that depend on it.

Above: Gila woodpecker
Below: Saguaros with arms are at least seventy-five years old.

Top: Petroglyphs, Signal Hill, Tucson
Mountain District
Above: Saguaro flowers bloom
and wilt within twenty-four hours.

SAGUARO NATIONAL PARK
VISITOR INFORMATION

《 OPEN 》 Park consists of two separate districts: Rincon Mountain District on east side of Tucson (Saguaro East) and Tucson Mountain District on west (Saguaro West). Both open daily throughout the year.

《 VISITOR CENTERS 》 One center in each district, open daily 9 a.m.–5 p.m., except certain holidays; exhibits, audio-visual programs, booksales

《 ENTRANCE FEE 》 Yes

《 CAMPING 》 No developed campgrounds in park; backcountry camping at designated sites in Saguaro Wilderness Area in Rincon Mountain District, with permit and fee. Nearest campgrounds in nearby county and state parks and Coronado National Forest.

《 SERVICES I FACILITIES 》 Restrooms, water, picnic areas

《 NEARBY ACCOMMODATIONS I SERVICES 》 Tucson, Arizona

《 INFORMATION 》 Superintendent, Saguaro National Park, 3693 South Old Spanish Trail, Tucson, AZ 85730; phone: 520-733-5153 (Saguaro East) and 520-733-5158 (Saguaro West); website: www.nps.gov/sagu

...all tell a complex story of two cultures learning to live with one another in the seventeenth-century Southwest, sometimes in harmony and sometimes in conflict.

Salinas Pueblo Missions
NATIONAL MONUMENT

The towering red stone walls of the nave of the old church at Quarai open to the vault of blue sky. It is a breathtaking sight and could give one reason to believe the structure was intentionally built without a roof.

Yet Quarai's church, La Purisíma Concepción, did possess a roof, as well as an altar, choir loft, sacristy, and bell tower. High clerestory windows permitted the sun's rays to stream into the great nave and onto the altar, draped with fine linens and set with candles and gleaming chalices. With transepts off the nave, the layout followed the traditional style of Spanish churches shaped like a cross.

Quarai is one of three Spanish churches that make up Salinas Pueblo Missions National Monument in the Estancia Valley of central New Mexico. The other two, Abó and Gran Quivira, are stunning in their own ways—Abó against the backdrop of the Manzano Mountains and Gran Quivira on a hill affording a generous view of the Great Plains. All three were built in the 1600s. All shared locations with thriving Native pueblos, Cuarac (Quarai), Abó, and Las Humanas (Gran Quivira). And all tell a complex story of two cultures learning to live with one another in the seventeenth-century Southwest, sometimes in harmony and sometimes in conflict.

When Spaniards visited the Estancia Valley in 1581, the Pueblo people were harvesting salt from the valley's ephemeral lakebeds and trading it to other tribes. In 1598, Spanish leader Don Juan de Oñate arrived with a band of colonists to settle New Mexico. He obtained an Act of Obedience from Pueblo residents, saying they agreed to "render obedience and vassalage to God and king."

The salt, said Oñate, was "one of the four riches of New Mexico."

But the Spaniards were interested not only in minerals. They wanted Catholic converts as well. Thus a hardy group of Franciscan priests went to the Native villages and asked permission to build churches and missions among them. With permission granted, the churches at Abó, Quarai, and Gran Quivira were built. Abo's first small church was built between 1622 and 1627. A new priest came and nearly doubled it in size, the ruins of which can be toured today. With Abó doing well, a missionary priest was sent to Quarai to erect the church there, around 1628. At Gran Quivira, an early small church was abandoned and a second larger one was started but never completed.

Other than the small supply of metal tools the priests brought with them, the churches were made from local materials immediately available. At Abó and Quarai, red sandstone slabs were used. Gran Quivira employed a blockier cream-gray limestone. Wood for the supporting beams came from trees that grew in the mountains. Timber was cut and left to season, then hauled in by wagon or on men's backs. Some beams weighed as much as 1,700 pounds. Indian women and children laid up the rock walls, while skilled carpenters completed the construction. The mission churches included a convento, living quarters of the priests and Indian converts who served as porters and cooks. Within the church walls, archeologists found kivas, special chambers where Pueblo people held their ceremonies.

Along with religion, the Spaniards introduced a new language, crafts, foods, and farming practices

Top: The towering walls of Quarai
Above: Wild four o'clock in full bloom

to the pueblos. But as drought and famine gripped the Salinas area, the Church's promises seemed less likely to come true. Doubt grew among the Pueblo people and they began to resist the Spanish influence in their lives. They also resisted the economic system that extracted tribute from them, and witnessed the power struggles between the priests and Spanish civil leaders.

Conditions worsened. Stores of food were depleted, and Apache raids exacerbated the problems. In 1668 some 450 people died of hunger and starvation at Gran Quivira. And at Quarai, Fray Diego de Parragao wrote that "Many are sick and some are dying. . . . We must leave, all two hundred families, and go north." He made the difficult decision to depart for good in 1677. Abó and Gran Quivira were also abandoned around this time. The people reestablished themselves at Isleta and other pueblos along the Rio Grande. The Spaniards were driven from New Mexico in the Pueblo Revolt of 1680 but staged a successful reconquest in 1692. Today, descendants of both cultures again live side by side.

SALINAS PUEBLO MISSIONS NATIONAL MONUMENT
VISITOR INFORMATION

❰ OPEN ❱ The monument's three sites—Abó, Quarai, and Gran Quivira—are within a 35-mile drive of each other and are open year-round, except Thanksgiving, Christmas, and New Year's days

❰ VISITOR CENTERS ❱ Main visitor center at park headquarters in Mountainair, open 8 a.m.–5 p.m. year-round. Also at Abó, Quarai, and Gran Quivira, open 9 a.m.–6 p.m. summer and 8 a.m.–5 p.m. winter; exhibits, book sales, information

❰ ENTRANCE FEE ❱ No

❰ CAMPING ❱ None at sites; nearest in Cibola National Forest and Manzano Mountains State Park

❰ SERVICES | FACILITIES ❱ Restrooms, water, picnic tables

❰ NEARBY ACCOMMODATIONS | SERVICES ❱ Mountainair, New Mexico

❰ INFORMATION ❱ Superintendent, Salinas Pueblo Missions National Monument, P.O. Box 517, Mountainair, NM, 87036; phone: 505-847-2585; website: www.nps.gov/sapu

Below: Abó, the remains of the expanded church

This land of jagged rock and volcanic cones is one of the closest likenesses to the moon that we can see on earth.

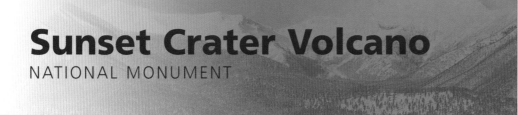

Sunset Crater Volcano
NATIONAL MONUMENT

Delicate pink puffs of seedheads on Apache plume stand out in soft counterpoint to the stark black cinder and basalt landscape of Sunset Crater. This land of jagged rock and volcanic cones is one of the closest likenesses to the moon that we can see on earth. In fact, Apollo astronauts came here to train in the 1960s to give them a good idea of their intended destination.

Sunset Crater Volcano stands out for other reasons. It is the youngest of some 600 cinder cones in the extensive San Francisco Volcanic Field of northern Arizona. Two major lava flows emerge from its base—the Bonito and Kana-a flows. Sunset Crater also is invested with great archeological significance—people were living in the vicinity when the volcano exploded and the event undoubtedly exerted a profound effect on those witnesses.

Sunset Crater was a Strombolian type volcano, middle-of-the-road in terms of strength and explosiveness. Earthquakes shook the countryside in advance of the eruption. Then, molten rock of more than 2,000 degrees Fahrenheit fountained from a mile-long ground fissure. Great clouds of fine ash billowed skyward, and liquid lava flowed like rivers of superheated honey. Cinders rained down—a half billion tons of them—eventually accumulating into the smooth-sided cone that now swells a thousand feet above the surrounding land.

Scientists believe the eruption happened less than a thousand years ago. From growth rings in trees used as beams in nearby Wupatki Pueblo, the date for the initial eruption had been given as 1064-1065; later research showed an uncharacteristically long life for the Sunset volcano, with

a series of several eruptions taking place during 150 years. Geologists now think the eruption was over in a matter of weeks, or months, at the most, and occurred sometime between 1040 and 1100.

While the final word still may come on the actual timing of the eruption, the other big debate swirling around Sunset Crater was its effect on the people living nearby. In the 1930s Harold Colton and colleagues at the Museum of Northern Arizona found a pithouse in Bonito Park, just downwind of Sunset Crater. The house was covered with cinders.

Colton went on to suggest that the 800-square-mile cinder blanket provided excellent mulch for corn crops, stimulating a land rush of sorts. Archeologists have since downplayed the mulch idea, noting that a century of good moisture following the eruption was likely more beneficial to early farmers.

A walk along the Lava Flow Trail at the base of Sunset Crater permits a close look at the fascinating landforms created when hot rock emerges from deep inside the earth. The Bonito flow is a confusion of blocky, sharp-edged *aa* (ah-ah), resulting when lava thickens as it cools. Slabs of

saw-toothed "squeezeups" rear up out of breaks in the ground. Beehive-shaped hornitos and ice-filled lava tubes can also be seen.

The crater itself is 300 feet deep. Though visitors can no longer go to the top, the almost iridescent, rust-tinged cinders on the rim are fully visible from a distance. "The red cinders seem to be on fire," said Major John Wesley Powell when he saw it in 1885, and so named it Sunset Peak.

SUNSET CRATER VOLCANO NATIONAL MONUMENT
VISITOR INFORMATION

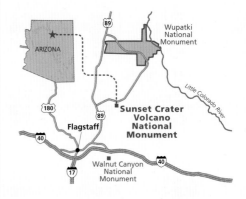

〈 OPEN 〉 Year-round (except Christmas)

〈 VISITOR CENTER 〉 Open daily (except Christmas) with extended hours in summer; exhibits, books, video

〈 ENTRANCE FEE 〉 Yes (also covers Wupatki National Monument)

〈 CAMPING 〉 Bonito Campground across from visitor center operated by U.S. Forest Service; closed in winter

〈 SERVICES | FACILITIES 〉 Restrooms, water, picnic tables

〈 NEARBY ACCOMMODATIONS | SERVICES 〉 Full services in Flagstaff, Arizona

〈 INFORMATION 〉 National Park Service, Flagstaff Area National Monuments, 6400 N. Highway 89, Flagstaff, AZ 86004; phone: 928-526-0502; website: www.nps.gov/sucr

Above: Geologists suspect the eruption occurred between A.D. 1040 and 1100.

> Professional excavations at Tonto yielded a fortune of perishable goods— woven baskets and pot rests, wood clubs, a beargrass cradleboard, yucca sandals, even a grass hairbrush.

Sinagua, and ancestral Puebloans. In any event, distinct adaptations to the particular environment of this transition zone appeared and are called Salado: adobe architecture, stunning red-black-and-white ceramics, and intricate cotton textiles. The Salado lived in the Tonto Basin for nearly 300 years, in a variety of settlements from large, walled villages out on the floodplains, to smaller pueblo-style dwellings on hilltops and in rock shelters.

Around A.D. 1300 the Salado decided to sequester small dwellings high up in natural rock alcoves above the Salt River. Today, visitors walk a steep trail up to the Lower Ruin, tucked into an overhang of Dripping Spring Quartzite like a falcon's eyrie. The climb gives a better appreciation of what Tonto residents had to do—going down to the river each morning to their fields of corn

Tonto
NATIONAL MONUMENT

The Salado manufactured excellent red-black-and-white ceramics

Central Arizona's Sonoran Desert may look like a formidable place to live—a lot of spiny plants and rough rocks, little evidence of wildlife, scant water, and scorching summer temperatures.

Unquestionably, the early residents here faced their share of challenges. But putting our view in a longer perspective, we begin to see that people not only lived here, they may even have enjoyed times of abundance and leisure. Apparently that was the case for the people known as the Salado, named for the Salt River that flowed through a broad valley in sight of the cliff dwellings now preserved in Tonto National Monument.

Archeologists detect the Salado culture emerging in this part of the Southwest around A.D. 1150. The Hohokam had preceded them by a few centuries, moving from the Phoenix Basin into the upper reaches of the Salt River drainage. Some see the Salado developing solely from the Hohokam, while others maintain that they resulted from the mixing of other major groups—the Mogollon,

and cotton, and returning to the coolness of the dwelling each evening, perhaps toting water back up in big clay ollas.

The Lower Ruin is a two-story masonry structure of about twenty rooms with a small "annex" around the corner, possibly built to house additional residents. The Upper Ruin had twice as many rooms as the Lower. Both were similarly built of quartzite boulders laid up in adobe mortar, the walls plastered. Main roof beams were logs of piñon and juniper, which would have required a trek to obtain. The woody ribs of saguaro cactus, stalks of agave, and reeds and willows were laid as latticework over the beams. The small doorways, at first square or rectangular, were later remodeled into half T-shapes. The thick adobe floors of adjoining rooms were at different levels, with stone steps leading from one to the other.

Professional excavations at Tonto yielded a fortune of perishable goods—woven baskets and pot rests, wood clubs, a beargrass cradleboard, yucca sandals, even a grass hairbrush. The cotton textiles were finely woven pieces of openwork, embroidery, and woven plaids.

After living in these cliff dwellings for about 150 years, the Salado left the area entirely. The reasons for their departure are conjectural— possibly related to climate change, oversalted fields, or discord among themselves. With the public attention associated with construction of nearby Roosevelt Dam, Tonto National Monument was created in 1907.

TONTO NATIONAL MONUMENT
VISITOR INFORMATION

❰ OPEN ❱ Year-round (except Christmas)

❰ VISITOR CENTER ❱ Open 8 a.m.–5 p.m., exhibits, booksales, video

❰ ENTRANCE FEE ❱ Yes

❰ CAMPING ❱ None on site; nearby on Roosevelt Lake and in Tonto National Forest

❰ SERVICES I FACILITIES ❱ Water, restrooms, picnic area

❰ NEARBY ACCOMMODATIONS I SERVICES ❱ Globe, Payson, and Roosevelt, Arizona

❰ INFORMATION ❱ Superintendent, Tonto National Monument, HC02, Box 4602, Roosevelt, AZ 85545; phone: 928-467-2241; website: www.nps.gov/tont

Above: Lower Ruin, built and occupied in the 1300s

Religious statuary, carvings, and paintings enhanced the beauty of the edifice.

Amado
Tubac
Tumacácori
Tumacácori National Historical Park
Rio Rico
ARIZONA
Nogales
Nogales
MEXICO
Sonoita
Patagonia

《 OPEN 》 Year-round (except Thanksgiving and Christmas)

《 VISITOR CENTER 》 Open 8 a.m.–5 p.m.; exhibits, video, booksales, courtyard garden. Built in the 1930s in Mission Revival style, the visitor center itself is an historical landmark.

《 SPECIAL EVENTS 》 La Fiesta de Tumacácori first full weekend in December; Historic High Mass every October; grounds open each full-moon night January through March; ranger-led tours of Guevavi and Calabazas, 11 to 15 miles from Tumacacori, are available only by reservation, call 520-398-2341 (fee is charged).

《 ENTRANCE FEE 》 Yes

《 CAMPING 》 None on site; nearest in Coronado National Forest and local commercial campgrounds

《 SERVICES I FACILITIES 》 Restrooms, water, picnic tables

《 NEARBY ACCOMMODATIONS I SERVICES 》 Tumacácori, Tubac, and Nogales, Arizona

《 INFORMATION 》 Superintendent, Tumacácori National Historical Park, P.O. Box 67, Tumacácori, AZ 85640; phone: 520-398-2341; website: www.nps.gov/tuma

Tumacácori
NATIONAL HISTORICAL PARK

Driven by religious zeal, Franciscan missionaries spent the first two decades of the nineteenth century completing an ornate Catholic church beside the Santa Cruz River in southern Arizona.

The mission, San José de Tumacácori, had been founded much earlier, in 1691, by Jesuit Father Eusebio Kino. When Father Kino arrived in January of that year, he found O'odham Indians (called Pima and Papago by the Spaniards) living in the valley. They prepared three arbors, he said, "one in which to say mass, another in which to

sleep, and the third for a kitchen." At the same time he established the Tumacácori mission, the ambitious padre also set up another upriver at Guevavi.

The O'odham were living in thatched houses, growing crops in irrigated fields, weaving fine baskets, and observing their own religious traditions. Father Kino's main goal was to baptize them as Catholics. Completing that duty, he proceeded elsewhere with his missionizing efforts, leaving the original Tumacácori mission on the east bank of the Santa Cruz. In 1751 the O'odham rebelled against the Spaniards, and two years later the Tumacácori mission was moved to the river's west bank where the church stands today.

After the Spanish crown expelled the Jesuits, Franciscans stepped in to control the missions from 1768 through 1882. Under the Franciscans, Guevavi and Calabazas (established as a mission in 1756) were abandoned.

Tumacácori gained in size and influence, but a report in 1803 deemed the church building substandard. Fray Narciso Gutierrez attempted mightily to correct its condition. With scant funds and with Mexican and Indian workers, a stone foundation was laid, and the adobe walls gradually attained seven feet in height. Work proceeded fitfully, but Father Gutierrez's successors pursued the project. In 1821 construction was renewed. Money from sale of the mission's cattle funded the addition of a convento with living quarters and a school. The church walls were doubled in height and under the flat roof were a 75-foot-long nave, choir loft, and bell tower with baptistry. Religious statuary, carvings, and paintings enhanced the beauty of the edifice.

Left: The nave and sanctuary were originally plastered with lime.
Top: San José de Tumacácori church

San José de Tumacácori was abandoned in 1848, the timbers were taken, and the church left to dissolve in the weather. But in 1908 President Theodore Roosevelt set it aside as a national monument. Preservation and stabilization efforts at the church, which began in 1919, continue today. In 1990, with the addition of the ruins of Calabazas and Guevavi, the site became Tumacácori National Historical Park. And in 2000, another 200 acres were added, bringing in the mission's orchard, farm fields, acequia, and land along the Santa Cruz River.

From the highest rooftop of the pueblo, situated atop a small hill, the view is of the looping green thread of the Verde River.

Tuzigoot
NATIONAL MONUMENT

The people who built Tuzigoot could not have chosen a more beautiful site for their home. From the highest rooftop of the pueblo, situated atop a small hill, the view is of the looping green thread of the Verde River with the blue bulk of Mingus Mountain rising to the southwest.

Whether the scenery was the reason for the pueblo's location is something we can only speculate about today. We do know, though, that construction began on this pueblo around 1000 and continued through the 1300s. The people who built it were of the culture known as the Sinagua.

Rough-cut local limestone and sandstone block were mortared together and laid up into walls, to form rectangular rooms. The earliest rooms were small, but as the pueblo grew and sprawled down the sides of the hill, rooms became larger. Ceilings, some of them reconstructed in the center rooms, had joists of juniper, piñon, and cottonwood beams, overlaid with a lattice of smaller limbs, reeds, grasses, and mud. The flat rooftops provided additional space for lots of outdoor work and play. At its greatest expanse, Tuzigoot consisted of more than 100 rooms housing more than 200 residents.

From the refuse that was deposited down the slope at Tuzigoot, archeologists learned a good deal about Sinagua ways. They grew corn, beans, and squash; made woven cloth and baskets of cotton and grasses; hunted with obsidian-point arrows; and manufactured plain pottery from local clays. The flowing waters of the Verde River and streamside marshes teemed with life—cattails, grapes, walnuts, turtles, frogs, fish, geese, beaver, muskrat, and mallard—none of which missed their notice.

The Hohokam preceded the Sinaguans, entering the Verde Valley from the Phoenix Basin around 700. Preeminent irrigators, the Hohokam dug ditches to usher water from the river to their fields, and continued their pattern of pithouse living. But by about 1000, the Sinagua had come down from the northern highlands and assumed dominance.

Tuzigoot was not an isolated site. An entire community of pueblos stretched up and down the middle Verde and its tributaries, including nearby Montezuma Castle on Beaver Creek.

With their strategic central location in the Verde Valley, the Sinagua were linchpins in an active southwestern trading system. They exchanged salt, copper ore, and pipestone for painted pottery, shell from the Gulf of California, and parrots from the south. The Hopi tell of a well-worn route, the Palatkwapi Trail, that led from their mesas to the Verde Valley, along which moved people, goods, and ideas since ancient times.

Tuzigoot was named by an Apache workman who looked out at Peck's Lake by the river and applied his word for "crooked water." He was a laborer on the 1933-1934 excavations of the pueblo, conducted by graduate archeology students Edward Spicer and Louis Caywood. They stabilized the walls of the vandalized, rubble-strewn site and rebuilt the central section. Artifacts gathered during their detailed excavations of the rooms were processed in the nearby town of Clarkdale. With the excavations accomplished and a museum built, Tuzigoot's value as a national treasure became obvious. In 1939 it was made a national monument. The old museum still serves as the park visitor center.

Above: The Sinagua built Tuzigoot a thousand years ago.

TUZIGOOT NATIONAL MONUMENT
VISITOR INFORMATION

‹ OPEN › Year-round

‹ VISITOR CENTER › 8 a.m.–6 p.m. Memorial Day through Labor Day, 8 a.m.–5 p.m. rest of year; exhibits, bookstore, museum

‹ ENTRANCE FEE › Yes

‹ CAMPING › None on site. In nearby national forest and Dead Horse Ranch State Park in Cottonwood.

‹ SERVICES | FACILITIES › Restrooms, water

‹ NEARBY ACCOMMODATIONS | SERVICES › Clarkdale and Cottonwood, Arizona

‹ INFORMATION › Superintendent, Tuzigoot National Monument, P.O. Box 219, Camp Verde, AZ 86322; phone: 928-634-5564; website: www.nps.gov/tuzi

Big birds of prey—red-tailed hawks, golden eagles, even an occasional peregrine falcon—often soar overhead. To Pueblo people, birds are healers and hunters, gift givers and messengers.

In a lovely wooded canyon in northern Arizona, people in the A.D. 1100s chose to build more than eighty small dwellings high in the shelter of limestone cliffs. As visitors to Walnut Canyon National Monument follow the Island Trail, peering into the small rooms tucked into alcoves, most wonder two things: How did these people get in and out of this steep-walled canyon? And what did they do for water?

The answer to the first question is that they walked. Shod in yucca sandals, these people, known to archeologists as the Sinagua, were up and down from the canyon to the rim constantly (and without benefit of the stairsteps people use now). They had to go up to their rim-top fields to tend crops, keep the birds away, and harvest corn, beans, and squash at the end of the brief growing

Walnut Canyon
NATIONAL MONUMENT

season at 7,000 feet elevation.

The answer to the second question is that they got water any way they could—a task that undoubtedly challenged their inventiveness. They placed large ceramic pots beneath overhangs to collect runoff, took advantage of bedrock depressions where water pooled after rains, and hauled water from the seasonally flowing creek. Obviously, they knew well the meaning of water conservation—every drop had to be carefully used for cooking and other domestic uses, and for crops as well.

Still, Walnut Canyon would have been a good place to live. The native Kaibab limestone provided plentiful building material, and the natural overhangs in the cliff walls were simply remodeled a little to make adequate rooms—more than 500 of them eventually. The builders placed most dwellings on south-facing exposures, taking advantage of the warmth of the winter sun. Wood was available for hearth fires—the thick black soot on the ceilings of the rooms testifies to years of use. Grapes, piñon nuts, wolfberries, and many more wild plants were also readily at hand.

Unfortunately, a good deal of Walnut Canyon's rich past was lost to looting in the sites in the late nineteenth century. Local citizens were stirred to action to protect the place, and by 1904 forest ranger William Pierce was stationed in a one-room cabin on the rim. Yet wanton destruction continued—even to the point of dynamiting in some sites. In 1915 Walnut Canyon received greater protection when it became a national monument. Soon, archeologist Harold Colton, who had named the Sinagua culture, began systematic work in the

sites. He, and archeologists more recently, have found tantalizing artifacts that bring life to the now-vacant rooms: cloth, arrows, pottery, cane cigarettes, a weaver's spindle whorl, someone's yucca sandal patched with human hair.

Between 1125 and 1250, the Sinaguans extended over a wide portion of northern and central Arizona. But around 1250, they left Walnut Canyon and nearly everywhere else too. The Hopi today call their ancestors *hisatsinom,* "people of long ago." And according to the Hopi, prophesies told them to keep migrating, until finally they reached the three high mesas where they live today. The Hopi still respect and honor these homes in Walnut Canyon and make regular pilgrimages here.

After completing the breath-catching walk back out of Walnut Canyon, visitors can stroll the level Rim Trail for fine views of the green corridor of the canyon bottom. Big birds of prey—red-tailed hawks, golden eagles, even an occasional peregrine falcon—often soar overhead. To Pueblo people, birds are healers and hunters, gift givers and messengers. Were they the message bearers to the residents of Walnut Canyon, telling them how to live a good life in this fair land?

Above: Walnut Canyon cliff dwelling, built of Kaibab limestone

Depending on wind direction and closeness to the source material, different kinds of dunes form. White Sands contains four styles— dome, barchan, transverse, and parabolic.

White Sands
NATIONAL MONUMENT

White Sands National Monument is an elemental place: gleaming white dunes stretching forever into blue sky, with cut-out silhouettes of distant mountain ranges providing a backdrop and some sense of scale. Plants are scarce, and animals keep a low profile. Texture and light give the dunes definition.

This field of sand, white as Arctic snow, is unique. The dunes are made of gypsum—the largest such dunefield of its kind in the world—

and they exist here because of a special combination of geologic and climatologic circumstances. Take some mountains, add an enclosed basin, a source of gypsum, a desert, and wind, and you have the makings of this 275-square-mile dunefield in southern New Mexico.

The mountain ranges that surround the Tularosa Basin contain thick layers of gypsum rock (calcium sulfate). Rainwater and snowmelt

dissolve the gypsum from the rock and carry it into the basin. The Tularosa Basin is internally drained, lacking a through-flowing stream that would otherwise carry the dissolved gypsum to the ocean. Instead, gypsum-laden water pools in the natural depressions on the Alkali Flat in the bottom of the basin, creating temporary lakes called playas. As the water slowly evaporates under the hot desert sun, gypsum concentrates and eventually is deposited in the form of crystals on the floor of the playas. Once the playas dry out, the exposed gypsum crystals break down into sand-sized particles, which the wind picks up and carries eastward. Nicked and scoured to an opaque white, the particles reassemble into the sweeping dunes of White Sands.

It all happens one grain at a time, a nearly unfathomable process. Yet on a windy day, of which there are many here, the power of this agent can be felt. Storm-force gales in excess of fifty miles an hour are not uncommon in springtime. Depending on wind direction and closeness to the source material, different kinds of dunes form. White Sands contains four styles—dome, barchan, transverse, and parabolic. The classic crescent-shaped barchan dunes and transverse dunes make up most of the active portion of the field. Finer etchings are then added, such as the beautiful ripple marks that sidewind across the dune surface.

The dunefield is active, always moving, always evolving. Sand is constantly being picked up and rearranged, the dunes reforming and rebuilding, advancing incessantly and halting only on the farthest fringes where plants have managed to secure the sand. The low areas between the active dunes are often covered by a soil crust composed of cyanobacteria and other microorganisms.

The wind draws ripple patterns across the dunes.

This biological crust stabilizes the soil, retains water, and provides nutrients to plants growing in the dunefield.

A few trees and shrubs manage to hold on amid the mobile dunes. To do so, some put themselves on pedestals. Shrubs such as rosemarymint and skunkbush elongate their stems to outgrow a dune. The pedestals form around their many roots, leaving the plants standing on hardened areas as the dunes move on. The yucca also rises above it all by elongating stems and trunks. Gypsum offers a limited menu of nutrients to plants, but a few, such as gyp nama, not only tolerate but actually need gypsum for growth.

Animals use coloration and behavior to survive in this monochromatic world. Cowles prairie lizards and bleached earless lizards have evolved whitish coloring, perfect camouflage on the dunes, while the plains pocket mouse lives life as a platinum blonde. Insects such as camel crickets, tiger beetles, and snout beetles are nearly white or transparent. Pocket gophers live underground, and kit foxes burrow into the gypsum pedestals on which shrubs perch. Signs of their nocturnal movements are recorded in the embroidery of their tracks on the dunes in the morning.

Early hunters and farmers inhabited the Tularosa Basin for thousands of years. Then Mescalero Apache came on the scene, and all the mountains of the region were part of their homeland. In 1864 the U.S. Army rounded up the Apache and moved them out, but they finally returned to a reservation east of White Sands. Spanish settlers and Anglos—including rancher Oliver Lee and a sheriff named Pat Garrett—began to settle the area. By the early twentieth century, health seekers were coming to the desert, among them Tom Charles. "Mr. White Sands," as he was known, was a prime mover in the effort to protect the dunes. Charles' campaign bore fruit when President Herbert Hoover proclaimed White Sands National Monument in 1933. With World War II, the military arrived. In 1945, the nation's first atomic bomb was tested sixty-five miles away at the Trinity site. Today, the western half of the national monument is operated in cooperation with the White Sands Missile Range.

WHITE SANDS NATIONAL MONUMENT
VISITOR INFORMATION

❰ OPEN ❱ Year-round, except Christmas

❰ VISITOR CENTER ❱ 8 a.m.–7 p.m. Memorial Day through Labor Day, 8 a.m.– 5 p.m. rest of year; exhibits, bookstore, gift shop, information on ranger-led walks and special tours to Lake Lucero

❰ ENTRANCE FEE ❱ Yes

❰ CAMPING ❱ No developed campground, but designated backcountry campsites in dunefield can be reached on foot; primitive, no facilities. Register in person at visitor center by an hour before sunset.

❰ SERVICES | FACILITIES ❱ Restrooms, water at visitor center, picnic area, snacks at gift shop

❰ NEARBY ACCOMMODATIONS | SERVICES ❱ Alamogordo, New Mexico

❰ INFORMATION ❱ Superintendent, White Sands National Monument, P.O. Box 1086, Holloman Air Force Base, NM 88330; phone: 505-679-2599 or 505-479-6124; website: www.nps.gov/whsa

Opposite top: Soaptree yucca
Left: Sand dunes overtake Río Grande cottonwoods.

To people living here a millennium ago, the thing that mattered most besides water was where corn would grow.

Wupatki
NATIONAL MONUMENT

A hot dry wind blows across the Painted Desert in northern Arizona. But the east-facing rooms of Wupatki Pueblo are already in the shade, even as the sun still burns high in the late afternoon sky. The people who built this striking three-story stone building must have had some reason for locating where they did. A spring flowed nearby, which partly explains it. But by and large water has always been a scarce commodity in this semi-

arid land. In fact, Wupatki's builders are people known to archeologists as the Sinagua, which translates from Spanish as "without water."

To people living here a millennium ago, the thing that mattered most besides water was where corn would grow. Though seemingly simple on the surface, this consideration is filled with subtlety. A gain of only a thousand feet in elevation, for example, meant eleven inches of rain a year

instead of seven. And for the Sinagua, that meant the difference between a full belly or an empty one from one year to the next.

Compared to the higher, moister juniper country to the west, the saltbush desert around Wupatki Pueblo would have been marginal for growing corn. Yet the Sinaguans did grow corn here and throughout the 56 square miles that are now Wupatki National Monument. Agricultural features have been found over nearly every square mile, thousands of them, leading one archeologist to call Wupatki "one big field."

In the center of it all, the Sinaguans erected the elegant Wupatki Pueblo. A walk around the structure is the best way to appreciate the labor it required. Builders laid flat slabs of terra-cotta sandstone in mortar and chinked them with smaller stones; in places, the banded rock walls are reminiscent of the masonry architecture at Chaco Canyon in New Mexico. Wupatki's builders took advantage of the native sandstone bedrock, fitting rooms on and around huge boulders. Archeologists discern several construction phases at the pueblo. The earliest section was begun in the A.D. 1130s. Then the pueblo burned around the year 1145. Construction resumed, until nearly 100 rooms had been added. Around A.D. 1250, most everyone left Wupatki, likely resettling on the Hopi Mesas to the east, and at Zuni and other pueblos in New Mexico.

In front of Wupatki Pueblo is a separate, un-roofed, circular space, an amphitheater that may have been a place for community gatherings. A few hundred yards farther down the hill is an elliptical, masonry ballcourt like ones found farther south in the Hohokam region of Arizona. Next to the ballcourt is a delightful feature, a blowhole

Above: Wukoki, another large pueblo, occupied in the 1100s
Left: Sandstone formations with the San Francisco Peaks in the background

in the ground where air moves in and out with changes in atmospheric pressure. The Hopi say it is the breath of Yaapontsa, the wind spirit.

Still the question remains: why was the largest pueblo within a fifty-mile radius located in one of the least favorable areas for farming? Artifacts found in Wupatki Pueblo may provide some answers. Several rooms contained the bones and feathers of more than forty macaws and parrots, more than have been found at any other single site in the Southwest. Also, much of the floor space was given over to benches, and none of the ground-floor rooms had doors. Wupatki Pueblo's size and visibility in the landscape have led some archeologists to suggest that it was more than just a simple apartment house. The pueblo may have been located and built as a way to claim rights to that precious farmland.

Wupatki was at the farthest northern edge of Sinagua territory. It stood at the intersection of several cultures—the ancestral Puebloans of the Kayenta area to the northeast, the Cohonina from the west, and Hohokam from the south. The eruption of Sunset Crater likely played some role in bringing people into the area. The cinder mulch that blew in from eighteen miles away may have enhanced the ability to grow crops, but so did a century of favorable precipitation following the eruption.

Visits to other excavated sites in Wupatki National Monument will only heighten the mystery—to nearby Wukoki; on to the Citadel, high on a hill overlooking a fault-formed basin called a graben; and finally to Lomaki and Box Canyon, structures built over deep cracks in the earth with the glorious San Francisco Peaks on the southern horizon.

WUPATKI NATIONAL MONUMENT
VISITOR INFORMATION

《 OPEN 》 Year-round, except Christmas

《 VISITOR CENTER 》 Open daily (except Christmas) with extended hours in summer; exhibits, video, books. Sites close at dark

《 ENTRANCE FEE 》 Yes (also covers Sunset Crater)

《 CAMPING 》 None in park; nearest is Bonito Campground near Sunset Crater

《 SERVICES | FACILITIES 》 Restrooms, water, picnic tables; also picnic area at Doney Mountain along park entrance road

《 NEARBY ACCOMMODATIONS | SERVICES 》 Full services in Flagstaff and Cameron, Arizona

《 INFORMATION 》 National Park Service, Flagstaff Area National Monuments, 6400 N. Highway 89, Flagstaff, AZ 86004; phone: 928-679-2365; website: www.nps.gov/wupa

Right: Petroglyphs in the Wupatki backcountry
Below: Wupatki Pueblo after a winter storm

Always Zion is a place of discovery and enchantment, a place worthy of worship.

Zion
NATIONAL PARK

assumes a mind of her own, with flows a hundred times normal. These high volumes of water energize the Virgin's true erosive power, a fact that Isaac Behunin and other Mormon settlers soon learned the hard way, when their homes and farms were routinely washed away. Erosion continues, with big landslides periodically spilling across the river.

Majestic vertical walls of vermilion and cream enclose the river on both sides. Here the Navajo Sandstone reaches its greatest expression—more than 2,000 feet thick in the formation known as West Temple. The Navajo is a rock borne of wind, formed from sand dunes in a desert that covered thousands of square miles back in the Jurassic, some 180 to 190 million years ago. It is nearly pure quartz sandstone, with elegant sweeps of crossbeds that preserve ancient wind directions. Herbert Gregory, the geologist who named the Navajo Sandstone in 1915, wrote that the rock is "everywhere a cliff maker. The explorer soon learns that the way by which he entered a canyon may be the only mode of exit."

With elevation ranging from 3,800 to almost 9,000 feet, Zion boasts a number of environments

"These are the temples of God. One can worship here as well as in any temple made by man." So declared Mormon Isaac Behunin, whose simple log cabin stood at the foot of the soaring cliffs of Zion Canyon.

It's easy to see why Isaac would have regarded the glorious sandstone formations as temples. Or as imposing patriarchs and alighting angels. Or as altars of worship, adorned with flowing springs and emerald pools. When Mormons arrived in southern Utah in the mid-nineteenth century, they met the local Paiute who called the canyon and the river Mukuntuweap, "straight-up place." In 1909 the federal government set aside land as Mukuntuweap National Monument but changed the name to Zion in 1918.

Flowing water in concert with hard sandstone created Zion's awe-inspiring scenery. The North Fork of the Virgin River starts high on the Markagunt Plateau, at about 9,000 feet, funneling for more than twenty miles through the park down a gradient of about 80 feet a mile. Over millions of years, the Virgin River was able to chisel down through Navajo Sandstone, slashing out Zion's popular slot canyon known as The Narrows. Downstream from The Narrows, as the river enters the softer underlying Kayenta Formation, the valley widens.

Through much of the year, the Virgin River is a demure, well-behaved stream. But when muddy flash floods roar down during summer storms, she

Top: Checkerboard Mesa
Right: Taylor Creek, in the park's
Kolob section

Clockwise: The mouth of The Narrows, Archangel Cascades along the North Fork of the Virgin River, and bigtooth maples in fall color

for plants and animals. Cottonwoods, box elders, and velvet ash line the river's banks, in soothing green in spring and blazing gold in autumn. Mule deer graze peacefully beside trails that lead to intimate grottoes such as Emerald Pools and Weeping Rock. Water ouzels bob and dip in the tumbling whitewater, and canyon wrens echo their joyous song. Mountain lions and lizards patrol the slickrock canyons. Trickling seeps and springs support hanging gardens of columbine, monkey flower, and maidenhair fern. Spike-tipped yucca and golden rabbitbrush survive on sandy slopes where water is less abundant.

Zion Canyon is eminently accessible. A road winds up from the mouth, closely following the Virgin River. The Utah Parks Company, an offshoot of the Union Pacific Railroad, began developing services for visitors here in the 1920s, including architect Gilbert Stanley Underwood's rustic Zion Lodge. People detrained at Cedar City, Utah, then boarded buses and entered Zion from the west. Meanwhile, the park's east entrance was all but unreachable until the Zion-Mt. Carmel Highway was opened in 1930. The thirteen miles of roadway and mile-long tunnel were a great engineering accomplishment, and it didn't come cheap—the project cost $1.5 million dollars, a lot of money in those days. But it opened the park's east side and afforded people the chance to make

ZION NATIONAL PARK
VISITOR INFORMATION

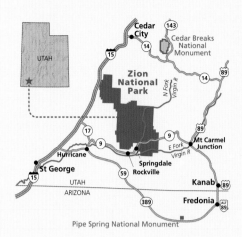

⟨ OPEN ⟩ Year-round

⟨ VISITOR CENTERS ⟩ Zion Canyon Visitor Center open 8 a.m.–7 p.m. in summer, shorter hours rest of year; Human History Museum and Kolob Canyons Visitor Center 8 a.m.–5 p.m. Closed Christmas; exhibits, booksales, information, orientation film in museum

⟨ ENTRANCE FEE ⟩ Yes

⟨ SHUTTLE SYSTEM ⟩ Zion Canyon Scenic Drive accessible by free shuttle only, from Easter weekend through October; closed to private vehicles. Shuttle buses depart at fre-

quent intervals throughout day from Zion Canyon Visitor Center, stops at several trailheads and other points of interest

Zion-Mt. Carmel Tunnel: RVs, buses, trailers, boats, and other large vehicles must arrange for escort (fee charged) through this narrow 1.1-mile tunnel on east side of park.

⟨ CAMPING ⟩ Watchman Campground open all year, reserve by calling 800-365-CAMP; South Campground, open April through October, first-come, first-serve; Lava Point Campground at north end of park, open June through mid October, 6 sites, primitive camping, first-come, first-serve

⟨ SERVICES | FACILITIES ⟩ Zion Lodge in canyon, lodging, food, gift shop, trail rides. For information call 888-297-2757

⟨ NEARBY ACCOMMODATIONS | SERVICES ⟩ Full services in Springdale, Utah, just outside park's south entrance; also Mt. Carmel Junction, Kanab, Hurricane, and Cedar City, Utah

⟨ INFORMATION ⟩ Superintendent, Zion National Park, Springdale, UT 84767; phone: 435-772-3256; website: www.nps.gov/zion

the "golden circle" between Zion, Bryce, and the North Rim of the Grand Canyon.

Zion is a hiker's paradise. The slot canyon known as The Narrows lures many, but it requires a real commitment of time and careful preparation. The entry for the full 16-mile hike is on top of the plateau. Once down in the sheer-walled canyon, there are few routes out and few places to camp. The hike requires entering chilly water that can be chest-deep and with a strong current; this is a deadly place to be in a flash flood. While Zion Canyon is the focus of most visitation, the park's 229 square miles contain endless backcountry to explore. The West and East Rim trails lead for many miles and connect with other trails. The Kolob Canyons district in the northwest part of the park is reachable by one dead-end road, and it offers more breathtaking redrock canyons and the 310-foot span of Kolob Arch.

Always Zion is a place of discovery and enchantment, a place worthy of worship.

Left: Echo Canyon, a slot canyon in the Zion backcountry

Copyright 2005 © Rose Houk

ISBN 1-58369-036-0

Published by Western National Parks
Association

The net proceeds from WNPA publications
support education and research programs in
the national parks. To learn more, visit
www.wnpa.org.

Written by Rose Houk

Edited by Abby Mogollón

Designed by Melanie Doherty Design

Maps by Eureka Cartography

Photography by

Paul Berquist: pages 13 (below left), 23 (below
left)

Michael Collier: pages 15 (above), 20 (below),
43 (behind park name), 56, 73 (above), 74, 80
(above)

Fred Hirschmann: pages 42, 63 (below), 68,
69, 77 (right), 83 (above)

Ralph Lee Hopkins: pages 6 (below), 20
(above), 24 (below)

George H.H. Huey: pages front cover, 6
(behind park name and above), 7, 8 (behind
park name), 9 (park name and below), 10
(above), 11, 12 (park name), 13 (below right),
16, 18 (right), 19 (park name), 21, 22, 23
(above), 24 (park name), 26 (park name), 30,
32 (all), 35, 37, 38, 39, 40, 41, 42 (park
name), 43 (above and below), 45 (park name),
46 (above), 47 (park name), 51 (below), 53
(both below), 55, 58, 59 (right), 60, 61, 62
(all), 63 (park name), 64 (both), 66, 67
(below), 68 (park name), 71 (park name and
below), 72 (both), 73 (park name and below),
76 (all), 77 (left), 78, 79 (park name), 82
(above), 83 (below), 84 (above), 85 (above and
below left)

JC Leacock: pages 50, 65

Allan Morgan: page 71 (top)

Laurence Parent: pages 1, 9 (above), 10
(below), 12, 13 (above), 14 (both), 15 (park
name), 17 (park name), 18 (left), 19 (below),
26, 27, 28, 30 (park name), 31, 34, 38 (park
name), 44, 45 (both), 49 (above left), 51
(above), 52, 53 (above), 54, 56 (park name),
57 (both), 59 (left), 60 (park name), 65 (park
name), 67 (above), 75 (park name), 77 (park
name), 78 (park name), 79, 80 (park name and
below), 82 (below), 86

Tom Till: pages 8, 15 (below), 17, 19 (above),
24 (above), 40 (park name), 46 (below), 54
(park name), 70, 75, 84 (park name and
below), 85 (below right)

Merlin D. Tuttle, Bat Conservation
International: page 29 (below)

Larry Ulrich: pages 21 (park name), 23 (below
right), 25, 29 (above), 33, 36, 47 (both), 49
(above right and below), 63 (above), 81

Printing by Global Interprint

Printed in China

Acknowledgments: The author extends
sincere thanks to all the dedicated employees
of the national parks and monuments in the
Southwest. To a person, they gave generously
of their time and expertise during research and
reviews for this book. Sincere gratitude to
Western National Parks Association, especially
Derek Gallagher and editor Abby Mogollón,
who shepherded the manuscript through to
publication with unfailing enthusiasm and
professionalism.